Stress Free
for Good

Stress Free for Good

**10 SCIENTIFICALLY PROVEN LIFE SKILLS
FOR HEALTH AND HAPPINESS**

Dr. Fred Luskin and
Dr. Kenneth R. Pelletier

HarperOne
An Imprint of HarperCollinsPublishers

HarperOne

HarperCollins books may be purchased for educational, business, or sales promotional use. For information, please e-mail the Special Markets Department at SPsales@harpercollins.com.

HarperCollins Web site: http://www.harpercollins.com

HarperCollins®, 📖 ®, and HarperOne™ are trademarks of HarperCollins Publishers.

FIRST HARPERCOLLINS PAPERBACK EDITION PUBLISHED IN 2006

Library of Congress Cataloging-in-Publication Data

Luskin, Fred.
    Stress free for good : 10 scientifically proven life skills for health and happiness / Fred Luskin and Kenneth R. Pelletier. — 1st ed.
      p. cm
    ISBN: 978-0-06-083299-5
    1. Stress management. 2. Life skills. I. Pelletier, Kenneth R.
II. Title.
  RA785L86   2005
  155.9'042—dc22   2004054157

15 RRD(C) 20 19 18 17 16 15 14

To Elizabeth
"Forever and a day . . ."

Contents

Foreword by Dr. Andrew Weil   ix

Introduction   1

1. The Birth of LifeSkills   19
2. Stress: The Good, the Bad, and the Ugly   37
3. Breathe from Your Belly   63
4. So Much to Appreciate   75
5. Tense to Relax   91
6. Visualize Success   103
7. Slow Down   117
8. Appreciate Yourself   133
9. Smile Because You Care   149
10. Stop Doing What Doesn't Work   163
11. Just Say No   177
12. Accept What You Cannot Change   193
13. No Time Like the Present   209

Afterword   219
Acknowledgments   224

Foreword

It is my great pleasure to write this Foreword to *Stress Free for Good* since it is truly a landmark book that provides clear, practical steps and "LifeSkills" that individuals can use to make healthy lifestyle changes. Making positive life changes is in fact a very difficult task for both patients and their doctors. Despite good intentions, there are far too many failures. This book is based on over twenty years of clinical experience as well as a major research project conducted at the Stanford University School of Medicine. Most important, it is based on sound science. *Stress Free for Good* makes using the skills of mind/body medicine as easy as I can possibly imagine.

Many books written about the modern plague of stress and hurry sickness offer a "break-even" approach. They provide only the means to cope with life. *Stress Free for Good* goes further, providing the reader with the skills necessary to achieve both optimal health and emotional fulfillment. Anyone can learn to use these skills, and readers are able to start at any point that works for them. You can begin with a meditation, or accept what can't change, or simply appreciate the present moment. This first step can then grow and be enriched by the other steps until the practice becomes an integral part of your daily life. You will find in these pages vivid examples of people who have successfully made life changes. I consider *Stress Free for Good* an important contribution to the field of integrative medicine.

Integrative medicine is now the fastest-growing sector of American health care. Despite continuing objections from the rearguard of the scientific establishment, many forward-looking doctors recognize the virtues of combining conventional and alternative medicine. As for American consumers, millions are voting with their feet and their pocketbooks for treatments other than those that conventional physicians are trained to provide. Integrative medicine is now clearly in the mainstream. Moreover, what is happening in this country is happening around the world. In fact, some countries— notably Germany and China—are far ahead of us in recognizing the validity of integrative therapies. In the United States, the National Institutes of Health has created the National Center for Complementary and Alternative Medicine (NCCAM). There is a new Consortium of Academic Health Centers for Integrative Medicine that includes twenty-five leading United States schools of medicine. Clearly, this movement is not a fad but rather a global sociocultural and professional trend with deep historical and intellectual roots.

In the United States, the change began in the 1960s with the loss of blind faith in technology. Up to that time our culture was captivated by a technological dream, the belief that science and technology would do away with all human ills, including poverty, illiteracy, disease, and, possibly, even death. Science and technology revolutionized medicine at the end of the nineteenth century and throughout the first half of the twentieth century, enabling us to make great strides in understanding human biology and intervening in cases of illness. Then in the 1960s came the realization that technology creates as many problems as it solves. In medicine, the created problem is expense—expense that has become unbearable. We are faced with uncontrollable costs of health care and an unacceptably large number of uninsured citizens. All over the world, medical care systems are breaking down as the cost of conventional medicine continues to escalate.

Unfortunately, the predominant American response to this economic breakdown has been a corporate takeover of health care. The people who now run our health care institutions are interested only in getting what profit they can from a damaged and sinking ship. Managed care is making the lives of many people, doctors and patients alike, miserable. Physicians resent their loss of autonomy and inability to practice medicine in the way they imagined it to be when they were idealistic students. Patients are increasingly angry about the impersonality of care and the lack of time they get to spend with physicians. This frustration is surely one reason that so many of them are seeking alternatives.

But there are other, deeper reasons for the growing popularity of the ideas and practices described in this book. When medicine embraced technology hundreds of years ago, it turned its back on nature and on all of the simple, inexpensive ways of influencing health and disease that previous generations used, many of which are still current in other cultures. It also lost touch with the most basic precepts of its own historical tradition. After all, Hippocrates enjoined physicians first to do no harm and to revere the healing power of nature. People all over the world are increasingly concerned about the damage inflicted by modern technological medicine, especially adverse reactions to pharmaceutical drugs. In deciding what to put into their bodies, they are inclined to go with the wisdom of nature. Like me, many of you are also fascinated by mind/body interactions, and interested in spirituality. You are disillusioned with a medicine that looks at human beings only as physical bodies.

For decades, I have been a strong advocate of integrative medicine, because I see it as the way of the future. It will bring medicine back into balance, restoring its connection with nature, refocusing it on health and healing rather than only on disease and satisfying the needs of consumers. At the University of Arizona College of Medicine in Tucson, I direct the Program in Integrative Medicine, the first of its kind, which is now training physicians and developing new models of medical education. A number of other leading medical schools have indicated intentions of moving in this direction. Most patients who come to our clinic, like most patients going to alternative providers in general, are paying out of pocket. This limits the availability of integrative medicine to the affluent, and if it does not escape that limitation, it will not have the influence necessary to correct the course of medicine. If integrative medicine cannot be incorporated into the reality of managed care, it will remain a curiosity rather than a mainstream trend.

It has been thirty years since I first met Dr. Kenneth R. Pelletier at a conference on "holistic" medicine in 1974. The holistic medical movement of those days was an early sign of the discontent that was building, although in the absence of the current economic crisis it was fairly easy for most physicians and medical administrators to ignore it or regard it as a fringe movement. However, both Ken Pelletier and I saw it differently and understood it to be the seed of something of great importance. Three years later, Ken published his classic international bestseller, *Mind as Healer, Mind as Slayer*, which defined the emerging field of mind/body medicine. That field is now a core element of integrative medicine, the one that has the greatest potential to challenge the underlying assumptions of the conventional system. It is also the component of integrative medicine that is backed by the greatest amount of research demonstrating efficacy for the largest number of conditions. Always drawing on mainstream science, Ken Pelletier's work continues to create the foundation for our understanding and applications of mind/body medicine.

For many years I have regarded Ken Pelletier's work as essential for the development of the kind of medicine I would likc to see. In *Stress Free for Good* he has joined with his colleague Dr. Fred Luskin, from the Stanford University School of Medicine, to create the definitive book on the applications of mind/body medicine. What these two have done is make the mind/body skills simple enough to be of immediate use to everyone. This book takes the work of Dr. Pelletier to its logical conclusion. Mind/body medicine is now available in an easily understood, reader-friendly format that is ready to use. Most importantly, Drs. Pelletier and Luskin have carefully researched the effectiveness of *Stress Free for Good*, so we know that it works!

Just a few years ago, I had the pleasure of reading an insightful book by Dr. Luskin entitled *Forgive for Good*. His first book demonstrated the ability of people to forgive past insults and injuries and improve their own health in the process. Now Ken and Fred have joined forces and written a delightful book of true wisdom with the power to improve a reader's physical, mental, emotional, and spiritual health. Most important, these two leading researchers and clinicians in the mind/body area have condensed complex ideas to create a simple yet powerful set of LifeSkills to use on a daily basis. These skills are easy to understand, can be learned very quickly, and yield powerful results. Finally, *Stress Free for Good* is based on decades of clinical practice and research as well as the most recent results of the LifeSkills program at the Stanford University School of Medicine, so they are actually proven to work.

Stress Free for Good contains first-rate credible information as well as practical skills that readers can trust. It offers believable stories of real people who have been helped. I know, because in my own clinical practice, many of my patients tell many of the same stories. Finally, *Stress Free for Good* will be invaluable to educators, to physicians in practice, to insurers, and to administrators and purchasers of health plans as they strive to help suffering individuals lead more satisfying lives. *Stress Free for Good* is an important work that I know will greatly enhance the movement toward a sound integrative medicine. Perhaps most importantly, the real benefit to you as the reader is that it helps individuals achieve healthier, happier, more fulfilling, and more productive lives.

Andrew Weil, M.D.
Director, Program in Integrative Medicine
Clinical Professor of Internal Medicine
University of Arizona College of Medicine
Tucson, Arizona

Introduction

We can't imagine that there has ever been a time when more people knew about stress or there were more books and classes on how to get a handle on stress. Hospitals around the country have classes on stress, meditation, and anger management. There are more counselors and therapists than ever before, and daily newspapers and monthly magazines all offer articles about and strategies for managing stress and making life better. Americans can even go to stores such as Target and purchase supplies for the practice of yoga, and herbal "stress tabs" are sold over the counter in every chain drugstore.

Yet stress is making people sick. They tell us they have too much to do and can't sleep at night. They tell us they have high blood pressure worrying about paying the bills or affording college. They tell us about their bad backs, their tight necks, and their chronic susceptibility to colds and flu. They tell us their stomachs hurt because they have to choose whether to work overtime or pick up their children. They tell us of their despair that they can't seem to get a handle on things. We hear of their anxiety and their fears. We see every day the toll that stress is taking on people's physical and emotional health.

Everywhere we go people tell us how tired and stressed they are. They talk about the strain of their commutes, of traf fic, of long hours at work, of the high prices they have to pay for everything (citing especially the enormous struggle to afford college, health care, and housing), and most poignantly of the problems they experience with spouses and children. Women talk to us about the difficulty of managing home and work. They tell us how tired they are at the end of the day. Men talk to us about managing home and work and how worn out they are. Children let us see that childhood isn't as simple as it once was, and adolescents have a full vocabulary of stress.

We all have so much to distract us and so little time. Everywhere you look Americans are bombarded with infor- mation and surrounded by incessant advertising. You can get the news on your cell phone or Palm Pilot or e-mails on your BlackBerry any time of the day or night. Everyone appears rushed, and the claim of distinction in too many conversa- tions is who is the busiest. Not who is the happiest or who is the most fulfilled, but who is the busiest! Who can get the most done in the least time earns the current badge of honor.

Cole Porter's lyrics perhaps work better now than when they were written seventy years ago: "The world has gone mad today, and good is bad today and black is white today." Instead of confidently dealing with the daily hassles, the struggle to make sense out of life, too many of us are buried under an avalanche of stress. The result is that our relation- ships, health, and emotional well-being continue to suffer.

Why, with information about stress readily available and people so comfortable talking about how to manage stress, are so many of us feeling overwhelmed and worn out? Why are so many people failing at their marriages, struggling with their children, and stressed at work? Why are so many people plagued by chronic back pain, headaches, and/or exhaustion? The answer is that they haven't learned how to develop the necessary LifeSkills. This book will teach you how to do this. That's why in a world awash in stress-talk we're so convinced that another book on the subject—*this* book—is necessary.

We have created the Stress Free program, outlined here in *Stress Free for Good*, to help you get a handle on your stress and improve your life. We know you can have better relationships. With this book we will help you find greater peace and even begin to experience the H word (happiness). We are here to tell you that most of your suffering is optional, that *Stress Free for Good* has arrived and is now at your service.

We wrote this book in order to address the reality of twenty-first-century America. People are tired, irritable, overwhelmed, and overworked. The good news is that we have created and now offer each of you a life-preserver.

Stress Free for Good presents ten scientifically proven LifeSkills to reduce stress and increase happiness. These skills are clear, simple, and direct. They work. They lead to less distress and they give you back your life. The practice of the specific LifeSkills leads to what we call the optimal performance zone—that state of mind and health where we can successfully handle the everyday hassles we all encounter. We will fully describe your optimal performance zone in Chapter 2, but for now we want to let you know that every single person has a body and mind that can function with power and grace, and practice of LifeSkills helps you find that zone with greater and greater ease.

Over the past seven years we have developed and refined these practices for stress management and emotional competence. They have been tested both in rigorous research trials with hundreds of people and in clinics throughout the United States. Together we have more than forty years of clinical and research experience in the arena of stress management and developing emotional well-being. Working together, we accomplished something that has never been done successfully: we created a set of simple and teachable stress management skills. These simple skills not only will help you manage stress but will help you become happier and improve your sense of emotional well-being. Just because these LifeSkills can be taught simply and learned easily doesn't mean they're watered down. On the contrary, they contain some of the deepest, most powerful wisdom humankind has accumulated over the centuries.

Both of us, as scientists and clinicians, had to know that these LifeSkills actually help people before we could promote their use. We had to know we were successful, based both on research and on the use of LifeSkills with actual individuals from all over the country. Over these past seven years we conducted the research and taught the skills to both medical and non-medical individuals, and the evidence is now clear: the *Stress Free for Good* program works.

Everyone has struggles in their lives. Everyone faces stress and everyone can benefit from developing better coping ability. *Stress Free for Good* is designed for use in our daily life. The specific LifeSkills are easy to teach, they're user-friendly, and they fill a need in a world where stress and emotional confusion are rampant and time is limited.

We have deliberately emphasized that these LifeSkills can be learned in ten minutes, can be practiced in less than a minute, and work in less than ten seconds. It's important for many reasons to have them be practical in our time-pressured world of job deadlines, soccer schedules, and endless airport security lines. We know how little time you have and how precious that time is.

Let's consider for a moment the impact of ubiquitous television advertising. If you step back from the content of any particular commercial, you will quickly see a very common pattern. Within thirty seconds, most ads complete the following sequence. First, they describe a particular problem—one that most often involves loneliness or social isolation. That unfortunate state, the consumer is then told, is due to a particular problem such as yellow teeth, bad breath, headaches, back pain, the social disdain that comes from driving a boring automobile, or even a new disease like "the blahs." Not surprisingly, these terrible conditions are magically and instantaneously made better by the particular product, such as aspirin, new clothes, a fast-cornering vehicle more suited for desert combat than a mid-city traffic jam, or a new drug that direct-to-consumer drug ads get patients to pressure their doctors to prescribe.

At the end of the commercial, the person featured is transformed by this external product. That initially unhappy and isolated person is now in a vital, idyllic state, grinning like a Cheshire cat because he or she is now the center of everyone's attention and the envy of all those other unhappy friends and colleagues. This message is hammered out at us dozens of times per evening of TV viewing, hundreds of times a week, and thousands of times in our lifetimes. If you don't think that message has a major impact on our lives . . . think again.

The falsehood that all of life's problems can be resolved by one particular thing is evident. However, there's a less obvious falsehood that is even more dangerous: the solution always resides *outside* ourselves in an external product, process, cosmetic, toothpaste, or whatever else is being sold in that thirty-second version of Nirvana.

We are bombarded with the message that inner satisfaction is the result of our purchases and external rewards. That new car or new computer will be just the thing to bring us that elusive satisfaction. And this leads to stress. The more we chase after these external phantoms, the more frustrated we become as we realize that these things don't get us any closer to happiness or life satisfaction. In fact, the emptiness we feel in the continual disappointment adds to our levels of frustration and stress. This can become a never-ending cycle of blind consumerism that has the capacity to spread into all areas of life: our unhappiness leads to the acquisition of an external token of happiness, which leads to more unhappiness, and then we start again. This book will prove to you that peace of mind costs you nothing and is independent of any product of the moment. Helping you to recognize that the solution to your problems lies inside of you is one of our purposes in writing this book.

What lies dormant in too many of us is the willingness to practice what we know is best for us. When we teach, we remind ourselves that in real estate there are three words that matter more than any others. They are . . . "location, location, location." This means that no matter how pretty the house or how perfectly it is priced, if the house is in a bad location it will be difficult to sell. Prospective sellers can read many books that describe how to make their house desirable and can think wonderful thoughts about the money they will make on the sale, but if the house isn't in a good neighborhood, that difficulty will trump any good ideas.

When it comes to creating better emotional well-being, the three words that matter more than any others are . . . "practice, practice, practice." In order to reduce stress and learn to handle life's ups and downs, it's critical to practice these LifeSkills. If you want to reduce stress, reading this or any other book won't be enough. It's *never* enough to simply *read* about a good idea. What if you read a book on driving an automobile but never actually drove a car, or watched a video on downhill skiing but never went out to a ski slope, or wanted to play a musical instrument but picked up your new flute or guitar only a few times? Obviously, you would never really learn the necessary skills.

You have to put those good ideas you read or hear about into *practice*. By the same token, if you want greater peace and well-being in your life, those results come from bringing what you read into day-to-day practice.

We will teach you what causes stress and how it affects your body. We will show you the pathways by which anxiety, fear, and anger affect your health and cloud your mind and decision-making. Throughout, we will provide a number of specific, effective practices that work. When you have a number of skills on your menu of responses, you can adapt them to the different demands of your life. Some skills work better for different situations than others; however, creating the experience of relaxation and the general skills to develop optimal performance are well mapped and always have a positive effect.

The real challenge is finding the way to make the directions simple enough that they are truly helpful. That means giving you, the reader, direct experience through guided practice and distilling the essence of what works effectively so that you will *practice* the skills. We have done this with our Stress Free program. We remind you that no matter how deceptively simple we have made each LifeSkill (in order to teach the skills in a brief period of time), each skill *works*, and with practice the effects are profound.

Mark is an example of someone who had read numerous books on stress, spirituality, childhood issues, and other topics related to mental health. Mark was a patient of one of the Stanford University Hospital cardiology clinics. He had atrial arrhythmia, which means that his heart sometimes skipped a beat and sometimes speeded up. This condition is scary for patients because they feel that their heart is out of their control. Mark complained of fatigue, of not having enough time in his life, and of experiencing a constant sense of anxiety.

Mark knew a lot about stress. He was well educated but still had a number of uncomfortable and intractable symptoms. The bottom line for Mark was that he felt crappy, too young to be sick, and too anxious to enjoy his family and life. In large part he suffered because he was not practicing the skills he had already been introduced to through his reading. Another way of looking at this is that he suffered because the skills had been presented in a manner that made them appear complicated and that demanded lengthy periods of practice.

Please don't misunderstand us. Reading about mental health and stress management is useful. Knowledge is power. Taking classes to improve your health is a wonderful and helpful way to lessen stress, enhance your well-being, and take charge of your life. We are simply asserting that books get read and classes get attended, but people rarely maintain their efforts after the class is over or the book is closed. Mark's problem, and the difficulty so many of you face, wasn't in the *learning* but in the *doing*.

Mark was young, in his mid-thirties when we first saw him at the clinic. Within the first half hour we explained to him the need for slowing down his life and for taking a few minutes out of each day to practice a simple form of relaxation. His response was a common one: "I know about that. I even took a class once on stress management. My wife is always telling me I have to get a handle on my stress." But when asked the obvious question—"Do you practice what you learned in the stress management class?"—he replied with a clear and resounding no. This book is for all of the Marks out there.

Our conversation with Mark centered on showing him how he could feel more relaxed immediately. We taught him the first LifeSkill during our first session and guided him in exploration of how he could incorporate this skill into his life. We cautioned him to go slowly, to not practice more than a few minutes a day, and to make sure that he practiced *every* day. During the subsequent counseling sessions, we taught him two of the remaining LifeSkills—the ones that were most relevant to his problems—and guided him in practice at the hospital clinic.

Mark made terrific progress. He learned to pay more attention to some of his habits and learned to slow down. He practiced relaxation for short periods daily and even learned to appreciate his wife more. His anxiety diminished, even when his heart was acting funny. He was able to lower first his cholesterol and then, over time, his need for medication. In addition, the occurrences of irregular heartbeat diminished.

We recently worked at the Stanford University Hospital with an elderly patient, Sarah, who at age seventy-eight had uncontrolled hypertension—in other words, high blood pressure that couldn't be effectively reduced by medication. While in another patient the doctor might simply have increased the blood pressure medication, this could no be done with Sarah because she was unable to tolerate higher dosages due to liver and kidney problems. At one point she had been told by her internist to relax as a way of lowering her blood pressure, but he never gave her any concrete suggestions how to do so. When we first saw her, Sarah felt helpless, unable to tolerate more medication, and abandoned without instructions about how to reduce her anxiety and tension. Not knowing how to relax, and yet being told by her doctor to do so, actually *increased* the stress Sarah was under.

During our first session together we guided her in practice of the LifeSkill that involves focusing on sensations of tensing and relaxing in specific areas of the body. We first showed Sarah how to practice the skill, then gave her step-by-step instructions, and finally watched her as she practiced. We did the same thing during her second session as well. Each time we saw her we instructed her to practice her LifeSkill daily. Within a few weeks Sarah's blood pressure began to drop into the normal range and she felt more in control of her health.

During our last session, we asked Sarah how she felt, and she stated, "My doctor always told me I needed to relax, but he never told me how to do that. Now I know how!" That's the main point of this book: it's the "how to" that we want to convey to you.

These examples of Mark and Sarah are from our clinical work with people who have cardiovascular disease. The Stress Free program has been shown to work both with patients who have and patients who are at risk for developing cardiovascular disease. Its simple strategies have profound physical effects and should be part of regular medical intervention for cardiovascular disease. One of the reasons we developed this book was to provide a simple reference for people in the medical field to offer their patients.

However, the Stress Free program was not designed primarily as a medical intervention. We called the ten specific tools LifeSkills because that's exactly what they are: they're strategies that most people need in order to navigate the inevitable difficulties of life. In addition, they're skills that, as you practice and master them, allow you not just to handle the stress in your life but also to experience greater happiness and satisfaction.

We assert that the Stress Free program is not just for people who are ill or depressed or anxious, or even only for people who are stressed out. *Everyone* needs to practice these simple skills to improve their ability to be flexible, to appreciate people and life experiences, and to make optimal life choices.

As we will show you in Chapter 2, there are specific mechanisms by which stress acts in the mind and body. There are also physical pathways that help people manage their stress. We want to emphasize that learning to live lives of greater peace and expanded emotional well-being transcends simply bringing unpleasant or harmful bodily symptoms under control. Managing stress is only a break-even concept; it gets you back to zero from living life in the negative numbers. But truly *busting* stress leads to happiness and enhanced well-being.

Stopping stress isn't the endpoint; rather, it's a means to be more creative at work, be more attentive to your spouse, see a grandchild graduate from college, and simply live your life to its fullest, undistracted and unimpaired by the preventable effects of excessive stress and strain. Inside you is a place of quiet, peace, and wisdom that you can learn to access. This place of equanimity and peace will improve your health, but that's not the only or primary purpose of this book. The aim of this book is to get you free of stress so that you can contact parts of yourself that are content and happy.

Perhaps the greatest importance of learning these LifeSkills is that they ultimately lead to a state of equanimity, to an inner, quiet poise. In this state, you're equipped to make good life decisions with regard to diet, exercise, work, and family, and to make constructive responses to the inevitable demands of daily living.

There is an apocryphal story that Dr. William James, who is widely acknowledged as the founder of psychology, had fallen into a very deep, morbid depression. During that dark time of his life, he managed to rouse himself out of his despondent condition with the realization that he had a choice between one thought and the next. He realized that one depressed thought didn't inevitably lead to another and that he could choose to redirect his mind. It was that infinitesimal moment of inner quiet and equanimity that gave him the leverage to move out of his crushing depression.

Despite the power of such a deceptively simple realization, we assert that it's equally important to learn to appreciate the good things that are already in place in your life. Likewise, it's important to develop the ability to slow down and get the most out of your daily life experiences. It's helpful to learn how to assert yourself and develop the ability to choose the right course of action in a particular challenging situation. It's valuable to be able to choose when to become upset over life's ups and downs and when to let things go, to recognize when gearing up to fight or argue is helpful and when a wait-and-see attitude is optimal. Each of these is a LifeSkill that will be taught in this book. Each skill contributes to your ability to be at peace and achieve optimal performance.

Kathy is a woman we worked with who was in radiant good health but who needed help managing her busy life. She had two young children, a high-achieving husband, and a demanding job. Kathy needed to learn to recognize how much she accomplished each day instead of focusing on how much was left undone. She never felt that she did enough, because there was always something else to do. She would go home from her day at work and face what seemed to be an endless stream of continuing responsibilities. We taught her the LifeSkills of relaxation and of recognizing the enormous good she was doing, along with the balancing LifeSkill of learning to say no when she was overwhelmed. In particular, honoring the amazing service she rendered to her family was helpful both to her body and to her mind.

Jim, another person we worked with, was chronically frustrated at work because he always had too much to do. He went home each day stressed, tired, and burned out. He felt chronically taken advantage of and was therefore filled with resentment. He liked the job itself, but he'd never learned how to say no when he thought he was being taken advantage of, nor had he learned to turn off the chatter in his mind through meditative breathing. Jim was given these two LifeSkills, and what a difference they made! He learned to stand up for himself, and he gave his nervous system frequent breaks during the day.

We have taken decades of clinical and research experience teaching stress management and emotional competence to thousands of people like Jim and Kathy, Sarah and Mark, and distilled the core methods into their essence. What we found at the core of our research and clinical practices became the Stress Free program. We present this program here through ten easy-to-learn LifeSkills that cover a wide range of emotional enhancement tools. We have found our selection of ten to be broad enough to help almost everyone who has tried the Stress Free program. The LifeSkills begin in Chapter 3 and are presented in order of simplest to most complicated. We have found this order to be optimal for effectiveness and ease of learning. We have taught the Stress Free program successfully to diverse groups of people in a wide variety of settings, and we have also trained other people to teach these skills. Through those successes, and through extensive research, we have proven that the Stress Free program works.

Many people are surprised to discover that they need to learn and practice such simple things as LifeSkills. We've been told on more than one occasion, "I already know how to breathe properly," or "I already appreciate the people in my life." Yet no one is surprised that a musician has to first learn and then endlessly practice scales to become proficient at the piano; that even an amateur athlete has to develop a training regimen; or that mastering any skill, from fine woodworking to surgery, takes years of training. You can look at LifeSkills as the building blocks to emotional well-being. That well-being is a much more important skill to develop than piano-playing and requires the tuning of your nervous system, which is infinitely more complex than any musical instrument.

Every time you practice one of the LifeSkills, you're either creating new or cementing already established connections in your brain and central nervous system. Each time you practice relaxation, profound changes occur that affect each of the organs in your body. Because of the enormous amount of information we have to process in today's world, our minds operate primarily out of habit. That means we do the same thing over and over, in the same fashion, until we choose to do something differently. Each of these habits is mediated through the action of our nervous system. With the Stress Free program, people learn to tune their nervous system until it functions in harmony with their goals and values.

The goal of the Stress Free program is to create positive change *for good*. We all want to achieve a state of equanimity, or inner balance, that enables us to respond appropriately to any inner and/or outer challenge. Like a confident martial arts master, we can all possess an inner poise and equanimity that guide us through life's challenges. In a famous BBC interview with Carl Jung toward the end of that psychologist's life, the interviewer asked Dr. Jung if he believed in God. Jung peered over his glasses and said, "I do not believe . . . I know!" It is that kind of certainty in knowing the power of your own set of LifeSkills that is the goal of *Stress Free for Good*.

CHAPTER 1

The Birth of LifeSkills

The Stress Free program consists of a set of ten LifeSkills. These skills include exercises (such as deep breathing, muscle relaxation, and focused attention) that will help you create a state of physical relaxation while remaining mentally alert, exercises that will help you remain emotionally stable while under stress, exercises that will help you experience greater peace in your life, and exercises that will show you how to recognize and appreciate the many positives and blessings that surround you. With the help of these ten LifeSkills, you will have the capability to respond appropriately and with intelligence to any situation that arises in your day-to-day life—and you will be happier besides.

We assert that these simple LifeSkills are for everyone. We're not suggesting that everyone is miserable or stressed out. Nor are we suggesting that every person reading this book is a failure at managing their lives. What we *are* saying is that life presents each of us with challenges almost every day and at every stage. Some of us are parenting small children, experiencing the difficulties of getting up on demand in the middle of the night and spending less time with a spouse. Others of us are working long hours to pay off a large mortgage or to put a child through college. Still others are mourning as their children leave home or their parents become old or disabled. In each situation, normal life is hard and we require tools to remain emotionally afloat and physically intact.

We coined the term *LifeSkills* to reflect the tools needed in order to manage the stress inherent in change, illness, loss, overwork, divorce, long commutes, and other normal life experiences. LifeSkills are practical, quick, and effective strategies that you can use anytime to optimize your performance and enjoyment of both work and play. You can learn these skills with regular practice in a relatively short time, and this book will take you step by step through that learning process. With practice, you can learn to enter a state of peaceful awareness in less than ten seconds. Each LifeSkill uses a phrase, found in the titles of Chapters 3 through 12, that helps you to quickly and easily remember your positive goal. This is our summary phrase for the Stress Free program: ten minutes to learn, one minute to practice, and ten seconds to work.

Our research and clinical practice confirm the effectiveness of this program in helping to reduce stress and its associated symptoms. Now it can help you feel energetic, be more productive at work, and reduce the wear and tear on your body. It can help prevent and reduce the risks associated with heart disease as well as manage the emotional and physical pain that accompany other diseases such as diabetes, high blood pressure, angina, chronic pain, anxiety, depression, menopausal discomforts, headaches, and stomach and/or intestinal troubles. It is important to remember, however, that while this book is helpful in reducing the disabling effects of illness (and maybe even preventing some illness), it is intended as a supplement to, not a replacement for, your regular medical and psychological care.

Every story has a beginning. In 1996, I (Fred Luskin) was a brand new intern at the Stanford Center for Research in Disease Prevention (SCRDP) of the Department of Medicine at the Stanford University School of Medicine. I was in the middle of my third year as a doctoral student in psychology and had spent a nervous few months hunting around for a campus job that would cover my $25,000 yearly tuition. It was difficult, and getting a graduate degree at Stanford, at midlife, was no cheap undertaking. At that time, Ken Pelletier had just hired me to lead the Mind/Body team of the new National Institutes of Health–funded Complementary and Alternative Medicine Program at Stanford (CAMPS) and I was awaiting my first assignment. Ken was the director of CAMPS and a clinical professor of medicine at the Stanford University School of Medicine.

At SCRDP I was trying to make myself useful when I wandered into the office of the coordinator of the HEARRT program (an acronym for Heart Education and Risk Reduction Training). This now sophisticated program of stress management skills, social support, and self-care instruction was designed to lead people to lifestyle changes that would reduce their risk of heart disease. It was provided to patients by skilled nurses who taught people how to lower their blood pressure and cholesterol, eat better, and get more exercise. Back then the program was just considering adding a stress management component. To begin this process, the HEARRT coordinator and I looked at a series of modules that Ken had developed for one of his worksite stress management research projects.

Over the next few weeks we edited these modules and met occasionally to plan our next step. Editing wasn't easy because the modules were designed for a different audience, one with a higher level of education than the group we were working with had. In addition, these modules required a significant time commitment from participants. Finally, the modules were lengthy and cumbersome.

Ken soon discovered that I had been editing his stress modules for the HEARRT program and was curious about how the work was going. One day after our weekly CAMPS meeting Ken walked up to me and asked, "What do you think of those stress management modules?"

When your boss asks you how you like something he developed and you've been working with him for only a few weeks and need the job for at least the next year and a half, your mind doesn't always run first to the truth. My temptation was to say that the modules were the greatest thing since sliced bread. Well, the first thing out of my mouth was, "The modules are too complicated and way too long." Knowing that I was perhaps being too honest for my own good, I added, "They require people to make a time commitment they may not be willing to make, and the bottom line is we need stress management tools that people can quickly and easily understand. Besides *that,* they're terrific."

I waited for an argument or some form of resistance. What I got instead was, "That's interesting; tell me more." To my relief I got a smile and receptivity to my ideas. When my racing heart returned to normal (more on this later), we sat down and talked, and the idea of making stress management and emotional well-being available in simple, bite-size chunks began to take shape. It was at this and subsequent meetings that the program now in your hands was born.

For over thirty years, Ken Pelletier's focus had been on understanding the complex interactions between body and mind, emotions and illness, aspirations and optimal health. He had written ten books on the subject, had made both audio- and videotapes to teach people how to better themselves, had developed corporate health programs for many of the Fortune 500 companies, and was a university professor. Over those years of teaching, theorizing, researching, and seeing patients, he had several "aha" experiences that brought him to realize the need for an effective, simple, and direct stress book.

I, on the other hand, had used several of the principles we then later incorporated into this program to design a unique and powerful forgiveness training that research has proven effective. My forgiveness research was done with people who had suffered all kinds of wounds. These ranged from the loss of a job to the loss of a child. I showed that forgiveness is helpful to people with all kinds of painful wounds and grievances. I found that stress management was necessary to anyone recovering from the unkindness of abandonment or the cruelty of abusive parenting or marital infidelity. Subsequent to that successful research, I have taught forgiveness to thousands of hurt people.

My studies proved that as anger, stress, and depression were reduced, optimism and physical well-being improved. I saw that as the hurt people regained control over their lives, they were better able to make good decisions. It's because of my forgiveness work that I'm convinced stress management and emotional competence are the keys to a successful life.

When Ken first published *Mind as Healer, Mind as Slayer*, in 1977, he had no idea that it would become a classic that remains in print more than twenty-five years later and in more than fifteen languages. In 1977 his thesis that mind influenced body and vice versa was a novel concept. He was a pioneer in the holistic medicine movement and was one of the first people to make stress management a household term. However, it wasn't until 1992, when Delacorte/Delta Publishers asked him to update the book, that he realized that although the basic sciences had progressed, the actual stress management techniques to achieve health were exactly the same as they had been in 1977.

Furthermore, he understood that these practices had been drawn from traditions that were decades and even thousands of years old. In fact, some of the meditation practices are actually over 2,500 years old and still relevant to the modern world. This is because the human body has remained the same for thousands of years. We don't relax and appreciate a sunset any differently than people did in the first century AD. Ken understood that despite the advances in basic biomedical sciences, what a person needed to do to relax and be successful remains simple. Unfortunately, not only are these skills timeless, so too are people's resistance to practice.

Later, in the 1990s, when Ken began working with postdoctoral fellows at the Stanford University School of Medicine, he realized that the question of why people weren't utilizing the simple skills that were known to have profound health benefits was still unanswered. It was during the give-and-take and exchange with me that we had a simultaneous breakthrough. It became clear that the actual techniques were never presented in simple, clear, practical, quick, step-by-step stages. They were never presented in a way that people could readily learn basic skills and then build on those skills to immediately make a difference in their health and lives.

We both realized that people could be taught stress management strategies in bite-size chunks. We grasped the fact that what human beings needed to do to relax and enjoy their lives hadn't changed in thousands of years. Our task was to take that wisdom and make the practice of it easily digestible.

With that goal in mind, we worked with a sophomore named Kelly who was struggling with the workload of her topnotch university studies. She came to see us because she was stressed about all the demands on her time. She had been the valedictorian of her high school and felt terrible about her current performance. Although that level of achievement was excellent by most standards, it wasn't good enough for Kelly. She was a young woman whose internal dissatisfaction was high, and we saw the toll that stress was beginning to exact on her mind and body. Kelly was nervous, and she complained of an inability to concentrate and a feeling that her life was getting out of control.

We taught her a muscle tension and relaxation exercise. We asked her to practice it with us several times and then finally on her own. We devised a plan that she would practice this LifeSkill regularly throughout her day. If she practiced six times each day, her total effort would be under ten minutes a day. From this brief and simple practice schedule, Kelly received an enormous benefit. Instead of drowning in stress and self-pity, Kelly learned to take regular breaks, learned to relax, and returned to her work with more energy and greater calm. For Kelly, while her workload actually increased, her improved coping skills rose to meet the challenge.

One of the most critical teachings of this book is that our Stress Free program isn't meant to be a break-even proposition. We want more for you than just returning to neutral after being stressed out. Just getting back to zero isn't enough. What you want (and we want for you) is to be able to approach life and its many unknowns with the skills to handle any situation with confidence and clarity. *Stress Free for Good* emphasizes and teaches you strategies that both manage your stress and further enable you to get the most out of your relationships and health. Stress management is only the first benefit of taking back your life for good.

Bill struggled to take care of his injured wife. She had been in an automobile accident and was recovering slowly. He worked all day and then went home to act as primary caretaker. Research has shown us that caretakers have, on average, a high level of stress and burnout due to the rigors of the job. Bill loved his wife and wanted nothing more than to ease her recovery. Yet he was crumbling under the pressure of helping her and the subsequent loss of free time. When we first saw Bill, his feelings of resentment toward his wife were just beginning, and with these emotions came the subsequent guilt for feeling that way. He felt trapped and saw no way out.

Right away we taught Bill two of the LifeSkills. First we reminded him that he was working so hard for his wife primarily because of his love for her, not out of a sense of obligation. We'll document for you later in this book the powerful difference your body experiences between doing something because you *have* to and doing it because you *care*. Bill had forgotten the love he felt for Sarah and remembered only the obligation. We reminded him, had him try feeling love for

Sarah followed by feeling obligation to Sarah to note the difference, and then had him practice feeling love. He noticed a striking increase in energy and well-being when thinking of his love for her and a sense of stress and failure when thinking only of the obligation. These differences weren't just in his mind but also in his body.

We also taught Bill another LifeSkill he would need to help handle this painful and difficult experience. Bill had forgotten to take care of himself during this crisis. He worked all day, weekends, and nights. He needed to be able to say no to Sarah and take time for himself. He needed to be able to trust that she would be okay. We taught him some simple strategies for saying no compassionately and helped him practice. The two LifeSkills together made an enormous difference to both Sarah and Bill. Sarah received the love and attention necessary for her recovery, and Bill was able to meet the demands of both his personal and his professional life without resentment or feeling trapped.

As you read and work with *Stress Free for Good*, you will find, as Bill and Kelly did, that the Stress Free program will increase your performance, satisfaction, and health by showing you how to transform stress into optimal performance. How to accomplish this is simple to read and understand, but it requires practice. The optimal performance zone is one in which you feel both physically relaxed and mentally alert. Regular practice of the LifeSkills allows you to shorten the amount of time it takes to move from your old tired, stressed response to your new optimal response. *Stress Free for Good* can be used to master stress and escape the trap of excessive wear and tear on the mind and body. This is not a fantasy or an empty promise; it's a proven prescription.

Stress can manifest itself in the human body in many different ways. The Stress Free program is designed to combat all the varied stress symptoms in the body—stomach distress, numbness, constipation, headaches, backaches, muscle tension, and many others. When the specific symptom can be observed during the continued application of a LifeSkill, we see people who have suffered for years suddenly improve.

We worked with Melissa, a woman in her late forties, who was a prominent model. She had been referred to us by her neurologist for "idiopathic peripheral neuropathy," or a numbness in the palms of her hands and the soles of her feet. Her physicians saw no organic, neurological, or other physical cause for the condition. Melissa told us of the high stress of the modeling world, with its anorexia, bulimia, predatory male executives and promoters, and intense competition from younger models. Her stress had become so intense that it was disrupting her sleep, causing her not to look her best, and affecting her stride down the runway.

To help Melissa, we taught her one of the relaxation LifeSkills. She practiced focusing on the feelings of heaviness in her arms, hands, legs, and feet to alleviate the numbness. This LifeSkill made her feel better overall, but she noticed that the sensation of numbness was beginning to creep up her forearms and also to the front of her legs. Despite this increased discomfort, Melissa continued the practice, because she felt she was making progress in a way that she didn't fully understand.

One night after leaving the clinic, she met a friend for dinner in a bar. She hadn't eaten all day and was feeling lightheaded. She ordered a straight scotch, and when it arrived, the pungent odor of the alcohol prompted an intense, spontaneous memory recall. She remembered something that she had repressed for many years: her father had molested her from the time she was ten until she was fifteen, during the years just after her mother died in an automobile accident. Her father was a prominent judge, and at the time she had been afraid no one would believe her if she had the courage to speak up. So she had suffered in silence all those years, and then had "forgotten" about the abuse.

What Melissa realized in the bar that night, when the alcohol's odor forced her memories to the surface, was that her father had molested her only when he was drunk. When she smelled the scotch, she remembered that she used to try to push him off with her hands and feet. During most of her life Melissa had tried to numb herself to the sexual assault, and the numbing took tangible form in her extremities.

When Melissa came to her next session and reported this memory, we asked her to practice her LifeSkill. Through this guided exercise Melissa was able to re-experience the sexual trauma, but as a relaxed and quiet observer of the assault. The repeated experience of relaxation while viewing the assault allowed Melissa to gradually feel safer and safer. Slowly, with some practice, Melissa became able to relate to her current experience without needing to numb herself. Before this, her fear of re-experiencing the trauma had been so overwhelming that she numbed herself to many experiences—even those having nothing to do with her father or with sexual activity. With regular practice of this LifeSkill, Melissa found that her numbness gradually subsided and positive emotions took its place. Within six months, not only had her symptoms disappeared, but her modeling career had improved. Melissa is an example of what we mean when we say that simply breaking even is only the first step on the path to well-being.

RESEARCH THAT VALIDATES THE LIFESKILLS

While we make some bold claims for the Stress Free program presented in *Stress Free for Good*, we have conducted research and engaged in ongoing clinical practice that substantiate our claims. We have demonstrated the effectiveness of the Stress Free program through those efforts and now present you a brief history of the research. This specific research has been conducted over the past five years and does not include the decades of work done previously or the large number of research studies that support many of the specific LifeSkills. We present this overview to demonstrate the variety of ways that the Stress Free program has been successfully used to help ensure that you will regularly practice these life-affirming tools.

As noted earlier, the Stress Free program began as an attempt to include stress management in the HEARRT program at the Stanford Center for Research in Disease Prevention. A comprehensive program of physical and emotional strategies to help people at risk for heart disease reduce that risk, HEARRT included assistance in blood pressure management, dietary counseling, drug monitoring, and exercise support and was conducted at various corporate sites in the San Francisco Bay Area. Our concern was that we weren't addressing the emotional and psychological factors that, alongside physical factors, predicted heart disease.

Our first attempt to include stress management was to schedule classes at the worksite for HEARRT participants. Even though we took the classes to them, people didn't show up in sufficient numbers, and after two years we stopped offering those particular classes. In response, we created the Stress Free program and began to test the specific LifeSkills available in this book. Our first research project established that emotional competence and stress management could be taught quickly and efficiently without the need for a psychologist or other mental health professional.

Each of the LifeSkills was delivered in ten minutes or less by a nurse, often during a patient's regular clinic visits. Each patient was given guided practice in the LifeSkill in the same way we offer it here in this book, and was sent home with a one-page practice sheet. Our methods were affirmed by the positive way patients responded and by the enthusiasm with which they practiced their LifeSkills. The nurses reported that the Stress Free program clearly made a difference in the life and health of their patients. In addition, the HEARRT program helped participants reduce their incidence and risk of future cardiovascular disease.

The next iteration of the HEARRT project included the Stress Free program as a core component of the heart disease prevention training. This project was conducted with poor inner-city people, many of whom spoke no English. Each of the LifeSkills was translated into Spanish, and from the beginning patients were told that these skills were an essential part of heart health. The program was quite successful and lowered patients' risks and incidence of heart disease as well as improved their mood and quality of life.

At the same time, we adapted the LifeSkills to make them part of a Web-based prevention program for pilots flying for a major international airline. The LifeSkills modules were offered in weekly installments and made available on a special Internet site set up for this research. The pilots were told that managing their stress and optimizing their emotions would reduce their risk of heart disease and improve their quality of life. They were introduced to the LifeSkills one at a time and asked to practice them. The success of this project showed us that our methods were effective even without a nurse to teach them.

Another project used the Stress Free program as a core component of a nurse-based education program to help people who already had heart disease. This study was conducted at various sites around the country with patients suffering from angina, a cardiovascular-based pain that's the result of reduced blood flow. This pain often accompanies exercise and stress and can be quite frightening. In this project four of the LifeSkills modules were delivered, one per week, again in ten minutes apiece. The study successfully improved the angina patients' quality of life by 10 percent. The patients continued to show improvement in well-being even when the training was completed—the last measurement occurred two months after the LifeSkills were taught. In addition, patients liked the program content, giving it a rating of 4.7 out of a possible 5.0.

The Stress Free program was also successfully tested in a series of three research studies with financial service advisors. This project used the LifeSkills modules as a way to deliver help to businesspeople experiencing the effects of the stock market downturn. Instead of giving everyone the same tools, as in previous research, we selected specific LifeSkills for each person to practice. Each advisor was given three LifeSkills and coached on how to use them in both business and personal life.

At this time we have the results of the first two groups of financial service participants; results of the third group are still pending. The findings are very exciting. Over a period of one year, two groups of advisors were each able to reduce their stress levels by over 20 percent. This means that a year after they began the program, they felt more in control and less harried, uncomfortable, and tense. In addition, they increased their experience of positive well-being by 20 percent, which means they felt more able to connect with other people, perceived a greater ability to experience pleasure, and had an improved sense of meaning and purpose. Finally, the financial service advisors grew their year-to-year sales by between 18 and 24 percent. Matched samples in their market group's year-to-year sales went up between 4 and 11 percent. This means the Stress Free program not only helped the financial service advisors to be happier and less stressed; it also helped them create a significant improvement in their bottom line.

Taken as a whole, this research shows us that we're on the right track. It proves that LifeSkills are sound and that they work with diverse groups of people in a variety of life circumstances. It indicates that we have successfully made stress management and the subsequent emotional competence teachable and available. Best of all, the Stress Free program did more than just help our research participants reduce stress: study participants showed almost a 25 percent improvement in the positive feelings of connection, peace, pleasure, and caring. These results suggest that people who use this book will be helped as well.

Before we instruct you in how to practice the specific LifeSkills, we want to teach you all about stress. We want you to understand its causes and risks and, equally important, to grasp the relationship between stress and optimal perform- ance. The goal of this book is to help you go from the experi- ence of stress to ready access to your optimal performance zone. After you learn about stress and its causes and dangers, and understand more about your body's optimal performance zone, you will be ready and able to jump in and create all the benefits of the Stress Free program in your life.

CHAPTER 2

Stress: The Good, the Bad, and the Ugly

It's a simple fact that stress is a part of life. No one can avoid it. Stress is the natural way we gear up to meet life's demands; it's the way we react to all the challenges of our day-to-day existence—mentally, physically, emotionally, and spiritually. Stress exists when you need to get out of bed in the morning in order to get to work and when you crawl back into bed in the evening before facing another day. Stress pushes you to cook breakfast to manage your hunger, and it pushes you to complain when your breakfast is cold. The problem is not with stress. It's how much stress, how often you feel stressed, and (most important) what skills you have to deal with stress.

Research has concluded that the events people experience as either uncontrollable or unpredictable are the most stress-inducing. In fact, some people define stress as feeling that things are out of control or that they can no longer cope with or manage what is happening in their lives. Research has also shown that whenever people are able to let go of the need to be in control, they feel happier, more fulfilled, and less stressed.

Just as we all have stress, we all have ways of managing our stress. Thus what this book teaches isn't something totally new to any reader. The reality is that in order to stay alive, we've all learned to handle at least some of the demands we face. If we didn't have those rudimentary skills, we would be dead. However, some coping mechanisms (like LifeSkills) work, while others (such as abusing alcohol and emotional repression) certainly do not.

What we will teach you is to become more skillful at managing stress, so that you can move from amateur to professional status. Some of the ways you already manage stress probably work well for you in certain circumstances, but some may not. As you learn about stress and how to tackle it, remember that you're not starting from scratch. You already do some things right (even if, as is likely, you do some things wrong). We are going to show you the surest, proven skills to immediately add to your repertoire.

Unfortunately, most of us don't reliably practice the stress management skills we already have. And even if we did, these skills aren't powerful enough for many of the situations we all encounter. Practicing the skills we will soon learn is one of the most effective ways to ensure health and happiness. For example, we want to be able to prepare physically and mentally for meeting the challenges in our lives. Gearing up in this way for a challenge allows us to do our best, like a professional athlete who gears up for a big game. That kind of preparation is good. It helps us meet the challenges of daily life.

The ten LifeSkills will be presented with full details in Chapters 3 through 12. Before we cover the specific skills, however, we want to teach you more about stress. To better understand the power of LifeSkills, and how best to use them, it's important to have a clear understanding of stress and its effects on your body and mind. We will describe the stress response, articulate the two different kinds of stress, discuss the physical dangers of too much stress, and define the *optimal performance zone*. Once you understand the underlying mechanisms of stress, you will then be ready to let the LifeSkills guide you as you work toward a Stress Free existence.

The bottom line: too much stress is bad for a person. Stress is a problem when the demands on your time and energy go on all day, day after day, without letup. You know you have a problem when you wake up tired or have a headache first thing in the morning. When you're in this state, you don't get the chance to relax before your body has to gear up again for something else.

Eventually, the tiredness and pain start to significantly drain energy that you could be using for other aspects of your life. They wear you down. Unfortunately, in today's modern world, this worn-down feeling affects all too many of us, all too often.

When you're in the middle of a particularly stressful experience, you *know* that it's getting to you. If your boss is yelling at you, for example, it's clear that something is wrong. No one wants to be criticized; no one wants to be yelled at. Even though you would certainly notice, in a general way, that you wanted to get away from such a situation, how often do you actually notice your body's reactions—that you're breathing harder, sweating more, and tensing your muscles?

THE STRESS RESPONSE

These body changes, universal responses for all people, are called the *fight-or-flight response* or the *stress response*. These physical responses to stress prepare us to fight an enemy or to run away to safety. They prepare us to deal with threats to our well-being or situations that are dangerous. This fight-or-flight response is what most of us think of when we think of stress.

Imagine yourself walking down a path in the woods. Suddenly you see a bear. Your heart starts pounding, your hands get sweaty, and your breathing gets deeper and louder. You're certainly not hungry, because fearing that you may be the *bear's* dinner has caused the blood in your body to shift away from your stomach to your legs and arms, preparing your limbs to defend yourself or run away. All your senses are on alert. If the bear starts to come toward you, you'll have to be prepared. You'll need to either run your fastest to get away or, if that option fails, fight your hardest to conquer.

To create this fight-or-flight or stress response, your body has to be able to gear up very quickly to do a lot more than it usually has to do. And it has to do so whether the threat is a bear or something far more mundane, such as a boss who's yelling at you, or being late for work, or sitting on the tarmac while your plane is delayed. You feel stress, and your body responds on the double.

In our daily lives, the most common things that cause us stress aren't clear physical threats like meeting up with a bear. Today's problems are different—things like that angry boss, bills piling up, traffic jams, unfriendly teenagers, rude customer service people, work deadlines, and family demands. These day-to-day normal events trigger the same fight or flight reaction in our bodies that the sight of a bear does— even though there's no real way to fight them or run away. When you're late for work, where are you going to go when stuck in traffic? Who are you going to fight when, after inching through that traffic for half an hour, you come to the huge accident that slowed things down? Are you going to run away from your own teenager? (I know some of you would love to, but it's not a good long-term solution.)

The reason stress is dangerous is that your body reacts the same way to an incorrect energy bill as it does to extreme turbulence in a plane. Your body reacts the same way to a rude agent when you're calling an airline to complain about service as it does to confronting a bear in the woods. In each situation your body gears up to protect you from danger. But where does all that gearing up get you? There's little that running or fighting will do either in an airplane going through turbulence or in your living room as you read your latest utility bill.

The stress response is optimally designed to protect us from direct, identifiable, and short-term danger. In modern life, however, most of the time the source of our stress is not direct but rather indirect, as in the daily hassles of a commute; not identifiable but rather a vague sense of being overloaded; and not short-term but continuing unabated for days, weeks, or even months, as in that frustrating commute or a serious illness in the family. In fact, for most of the modern causes of stress, running away or fighting would be completely useless. And this is one of the main reasons why our current strategies for battling stress don't work.

We too often practice our useless fight-or-flight solutions and wonder why we never get a handle on our lives. When this occurs over a prolonged period of time, our body breaks down at its weakest link in the form of a symptom such as a headache or a stress-related disorder (such as diabetes). In this way stress can literally become a killer.

PHYSICAL EFFECTS OF THE STRESS RESPONSE

The fight-or-flight response is the specific way the body prepares itself to face a threat; it's a perfectly normal and perfectly healthy expression—in fact, we need it to survive. Thus a well-functioning stress response is an indication of an active and healthy nervous system. Our body reacts with the fight-

or flight response when we feel overwhelmed, perceive ourselves to be in danger, or simply have too much to do and too
little time.

When you're experiencing the stress response:

- Your heart pumps faster to get more blood to your
  muscles.
- Your blood pressure rises as your arteries narrow and
  your heart beats faster.
- Your breathing becomes faster to move more oxygen to
  your blood.
- Your muscles tense up to get ready for action. This can
  result in a feeling of muscular pain and stiffness or even
  in muscle spasms or back pain.
- Your blood flow to the prefrontal cortex (or higher reasoning center) of the brain diminishes as more blood
  flows to the limbic (or more primitive) part of the brain.
- Your digestion stops so that more blood is available for
  your brain and muscles. The result can be an upset
  stomach or even "irritable bowel syndrome" or abdominal discomfort and bloating.
- You sweat more to help cool off your body and also to
  become lighter in preparation for a potential physical
  confrontation.
- Your pupils get bigger and your senses of smell and
  hearing become stronger to be sure that you have the
  heightened senses to perform at your best.

- Your arteries around your heart develop increased inflammation and strain.
- Your immune system, which protects you from bacterial and viral infections, is diminished.

At the same time we experience these physical responses to stress, there is an equally powerful psychological response. In order to engage our survival skills, we focus solely on the immediate danger. This focus keeps our attention on the problem at hand, but it limits our reasoning powers for finding solutions. For example, when a car is about to cross the divider and hit you, all of your attention and action are concentrated on getting out of the way. Instead of *thinking* about the danger, you *react* to it.

As noted earlier, one of the survival mechanisms of the stress response is that blood flow diminishes to the prefrontal cortex and shifts to the limbic system. While the prefrontal cortex allows you to *think* about danger when you're calm, the limbic system, fueled by extra blood during stress, allows you to *react* to it. As blood flow to the prefrontal cortex diminishes, electrical activity in that area becomes less coherent and less powerful, and the ability to reason diminishes along with it.

These mental changes are there to protect us in a threatening situation such as an attack or a fall down the stairs. They allow our mind to react to danger through automatic habits that occur rapidly without our even having to think. If a car is coming at us, we don't have to tell the brain to focus on the problem at hand or tell our breathing to become shallow or tell our legs to move. These are automatic responses triggered by the limbic brain to try to save our life.

Unfortunately, this danger-based focus often excludes other possibilities, such as being able to see another person's point of view in an argument. The fight-or-flight response keeps us stuck in our perception that we're in danger, because our attention is narrowed and our bodies are tense. How many of us have hurt people we love because we have felt stressed and uptight? The fight-or-flight response can keep us acting stubborn in a work or family crisis when what we truly need is flexibility and understanding. When we finally calm down, we find the right words to say, the right actions to take, that were unavailable to us when we were stressed.

On a psychological level, the stress response too often leads us to make poor decisions that limit our ability to deal with the challenges in our lives. For example, a stressed response in traffic to a person cutting in front of you is to get angry and lean on the horn. That may not only be futile, it may actually create more danger for you and your family in this era of road rage and the use of cars as weapons. Likewise, a stressed response at home may make us say the wrong thing in an argument and fill the rest of our evening with tension and bad moods. The bottom line is that the fight-or-flight response creates a rigidity and inflexibility in the mind that accompanies the tension and discomfort of the muscles and skeletal system.

While the basic fight-or-flight response is the same for each person, the internal and/or external events that can trigger this response vary. What makes stress difficult to manage is that everyone reacts differently. Some situations are stressful for almost everyone, like having a spouse develop Alzheimer's disease or missing a major work deadline. However, even in these situations the intensity of response will be different among members of the same family. Simply put, people respond to and handle stress differently.

When faced with a difficult situation, you may be the kind of person who at first freaks out and then calms down, while your spouse may tend to stay upset at a modest level for many days. Other situations, like being the center of attention, may be fun for you but frightening for your best friend. Thus (except in certain cases of extreme physical danger) we can't ever say that a particular situation is or is not inherently stressful.

You may love speaking in public and enjoy chatting with strangers when waiting in line; your friend may hate being the center of attention and not be able to stand waiting in line. You may find sitting in traffic stressful, even though nothing awful is actually happening, while your friend may not mind having a few minutes with nothing to do but catch up on news via the car radio. Even though objectively little danger exists for the person who experiences stress while waiting in line or speaking in public or dealing with traffic, the fight-or-flight response is initiated anyway, while the person who doesn't find those experiences stressful is unaffected physically. The fact that stress is a *personal* experience makes the learning and practicing of LifeSkills essential.

PROFILING THE TWO TYPES OF STRESS

The technical definition of stress is the amount of energy you need to adjust to the internal and external demands of your life in a given amount of time. Stress is the balance between what you have to do and the resources you have to do it with. That means something stressful on Monday may not be stressful on Tuesday, when you have lots of time and lots of help.

When balancing what we have to do against our resources, the resource that's almost universally in short supply in today's modern world is time. Although, as we saw earlier, what triggers stress differs from person to person, almost all of us are familiar with the stress that results when we have to do more things than we have time for. That's a common problem now, with more to do every day at home and work and less and less time to do it in. But time pressures aren't the only kind of stress.

There are two major categories of stress. There is the stress of being late to work and the stress of having a sick husband. There is the stress of one overdrawn check and the stress of a whole checkbook full of them. There is the stress of one argument with your spouse and the stress of the daily sniping that occurs in a troubled marriage. Although your body reacts with the fight-or-flight response in each situation, it's important that you can distinguish between the two major types of stress.

Type 1 stress occurs when the source of the stress is immediate and identifiable, and when the stress can be resolved in a short period of time. This type of stress is usually uncomfortable, but dealing with it is often necessary for survival. For example, avoiding an imminent traffic accident or regaining your footing while climbing a mountain is Type 1 stress. This kind of stress can also be pleasurable in many situations—for instance, the excitement you feel when you navigate a downhill run on a ski slope, hit a perfect golf stroke, or surf successfully along a large wave at the beach. The rush you experience in all of these situations is your body and mind raising your physical awareness through the release of the stress hormone adrenaline, which prepares the body for urgent action, and endorphins, which at the same time dull the body's sensation of pain.

If you think about it, your heart is designed to function continuously under varying degrees of stress. In fact, it's designed to last for a lifetime and flexibly handle many different situations. Your heart needs to speed up in argument and slow down so you can enjoy a sunset. Your flexible and resilient heartbeat, the result of the heart muscles contracting and relaxing, reflects the body's optimal, physical response to stress.

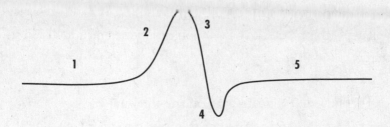

A single heartbeat as represented on this electrocardiogram (EKG) reading is a perfect schematic for the Type 1 stress response:

- Phase 1 displays your body's normal resting heart rate, breathing pattern, and other vital signs.
- Phase 2 displays your body's initial response to a challenge. A rapid increase in heart rate, breathing, muscle tension, and other vital signs occurs during the upward slope of phase 2. This is the visual of the fight-or-flight response, your body's method of preparing to defend itself or run away from an immediate threat.
- Phase 3 shows what occurs after the challenge has been met. Your body relaxes, and all vital signs begin to return to normal.
- Phase 4 reveals that your body's vital signs actually dip below their normal level to compensate for the extra demands placed on the body during phase 2. This is called *rebound*.
- In phase 5 your body returns to its normal resting state.

To illustrate these normal five phases of Type 1 stress, we will apply this process to a common situation, a near collision in traffic:

- Phase 1: You're driving on the freeway.
- Phase 2: As a car begins to move into your lane, you become alert and focused. Your diaphragm, a broad muscle below your lungs that helps you breathe, becomes tight, so you begin to hyperventilate (or take short, shallow breaths) to help get as much oxygen to the brain as possible.
- Phase 3: Instinctively avoiding the collision, you take a deep breath or give a sigh of relief, releasing the tension in your diaphragm.
- Phase 4: You feel shaky, jittery, and/or a bit disoriented. These feelings are the result of your muscles becoming relaxed and/or your heart rate and blood pressure dropping below normal to compensate for their increased level of activity during your near miss.
- Phase 5: You return to normal and continue driving on the freeway.

Type 2 (or long-term) stress occurs when the source of your stress is unclear, not immediate, and sometimes not even recognizable. Unfortunately, much of the stress you face on a daily basis falls into this category. Examples of common Type 2 stressors include chronic conflict with your boss or co-worker, continuous worry over your child's school progress, an ongoing personal health problem, and acute marital problems such as separation or divorce. This type of stress places very different demands on your body and mind than Type 1 stress.

Although when you experience Type 2 stress you're not responding to an immediate, identifiable threat, your body reacts as if you were because it can't distinguish between potential bodily danger and your ongoing dissatisfaction with your boss's carping and nagging. What you *think* is stressful *becomes* stressful because your body reacts the same way to an immediate danger that it does to the recollection of an insult from two weeks ago.

A diagram of the body's response to Type 2 stress is presented below.

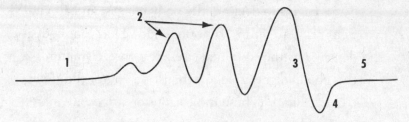

This response is quite different from the Type 1 stress response we saw earlier. The Type 2 response wears out your body and can literally kill you:

- Phase 1 represents your body's normal resting heart rate, breathing pattern, and other vital signs.
- Phase 2 includes a series of peaks and valleys that represent your body's response to a series of challenges. For example, you work in an office and on Monday

morning go in and face an unexpected deadline. This results in a rapid increase in heart rate, breathing, muscle tension, and other vital signs indicated by the first slope of phase 2. Once that challenge has been addressed, you get a call from your child's school saying that he has gotten in trouble. Just as you are digesting that information, your boss tells you the work you did was inaccurate and needs to be redone. These stressful experiences continue to occur throughout your day. Multiple challenges like these result in a series of peaks during which your vital signs stay elevated for an hour, several hours, or the entire day.

- Phase 3 occurs after the challenges have been met. Stress begins to decline, the body relaxes, and all vital signs begin to return to normal. However, your body is depleted by the sustained stress response. Symptoms of this phase might include exhaustion and/or the "four o'clock slump." These indications of fatigue are more noticeable after the stress response is over and you have time to reflect on the day and its demands.

- In phase 4, your body's vital signs dip below their normal level to compensate for the many demands placed on the body in phase 2. You might experience symptoms such as weak muscles (due to a depletion of energy stores in muscle tissue), disorientation (due to a slowing of brain wave activity as the brain compensates for the demands of the stress response), or a "let down"

feeling (due to reduced blood sugar levels and mental fatigue).
- Finally, your body returns to its normal state in phase 5.

As shown in the diagram on the previous page, Type 2 stress is the result of your body's healthy response to Type 1 stress that goes on for too long. Your body's perfectly normal response to challenges can be destructive when those challenges are experienced over a long period of time—hours, days, weeks, or even months. The longer this negative response goes on, the more severe will be your symptoms of distress.

The result of Type 2 stress is often physical symptoms of discomfort or the onset of serious complications. The symptoms typically compound with time: the first result of Type 2 stress may be tiredness; the next, after yet another grueling day, may be a headache on top of that fatigue. As the stresses go on and on, symptoms often intensify and become more severe. If the stress continues, your body can break down at its weakest point and develop illnesses such as high blood pressure or diabetes. Ultimately, unchecked stress will limit your body's overall ability to heal itself.

Here are a few common examples of what happens in your body as a direct result of unmanaged Type 2 stress:

- An increase in muscle tension can result in muscle tightness, back pain, and/or chronic headache.

- Changes in breathing can result in shortness of breath or rapid, shallow breathing (hyperventilation).
- An increased heart rate can result in an irregular heartbeat (arrhythmia) or a rapid heartbeat (tachycardia).
- Increased activity in the brain can lead to anxiety, racing thoughts, a lack of focus, or depressive symptoms when your body tries to recover from the stress.
- Activity in the intestines can become irritable bowel syndrome, diarrhea, heartburn, or even gastroesophageal reflux disease (GERD).
- Prolonged heightened vision can result in eyestrain.
- Increased inflammation in the coronary arteries can lead to heart disease.
- A weakened immune system can lead to increased risk of infections, colds, flu, and other communicable diseases as well as a longer recovery time when already ill.

Type 2 stress can lead to high blood pressure and back and stomach trouble as well as more serious conditions, such as heart disease or even a heart attack. Type 2 stress doesn't just go away and leave you alone; it's unrelenting. It keeps signaling to you that you are exceeding the limits of your mind and body and need to do something about it. If you pay attention early and take corrective action, you are likely fine. But if you ignore these early warning signs, the symptoms of the body will continue to worsen until you pay attention or eventually become immobilized by a stress-related disease.

When you experience stress too often or for too long, you start to feel the negative effects of Type 2 stress. The whole range of consequences listed above may not strike you, since the effects are different for different people. Some people feel tired, others feel nervous or anxious, and still others complain about extra irritability. Some people notice that they're sick more often or are making more mistakes at work. Of course, getting upset or sick every once in a while is normal. It's just when this happens too often that you want to look at what's going on in your life. Becoming sick, tired, and/or irritable can be a signal that Type 2 stress is wearing you down.

The connection between stress and our physical and emotional health isn't always obvious, but it's powerful. We all take for granted that colds and other illnesses have physical causes, such as a virus or bacterium—in fact, doctors now know that our bodies are *always* fighting off infections—but those disease agents don't bear full responsibility for our being sick. Being under too much stress limits our ability to fight the viruses and bacteria all around us, because it weakens our immune response. When the body's resources are consumed by the Type 2 stress response, we have no defenses left to battle *real* enemies within.

It's a scientific fact that colds and flu occur more often and with a slower recovery time in people under stress. Research has proven this with students at exam time, elderly people at the death of a spouse or friend, accountants during tax season, and military personnel during combat. The Type 2 stress response explains why people under stress get sick more often. It's estimated that between 50 and 80 percent of all visits to the doctor are for problems related to stress.

THE OPTIMAL PERFORMANCE ZONE

The *optimal performance zone* is our name for the state of balance and effectiveness that people have the capacity to create when they deal successfully with their Type 2 stress. The Stress Free program is part of the field of mind/body medicine—that is, medicine that looks to both body and mind for the causes and the cures of illness. An emerging body of medical research shows positive effects for the largest number of people under the widest variety of conditions with the use of mind/body medicine. Such practices are now gaining wide acceptance as alternative therapies within the conventional medical world.

While stress can lead to and/or aggravate a wide array of diseases, medical research shows that practicing mind/body medicine has a positive impact on cardiovascular disease (such as high blood pressure and congestive heart failure), insomnia, chronic pain, fibromyalgia, arthritis, and incontinence; improves results both going into and after surgery; serves as an adjunct to cancer treatment (alleviating nausea due to chemotherapy); aids in the treatment of allergies, asthma, dermatological disorders, diabetes, irritable bowel syndrome, peptic ulcer, ringing in the ears, and the breathing problems seen in chronic obstructive pulmonary disorder; slows the progression of HIV and AIDS; helps in post-stroke and post-heart attack rehabilitation; and improves conception and pregnancy outcomes.

It is because we each have such a finely tuned stress response and can suffer the effects of Type 2 stress that the converse is also true: finding our optimal performance zone and soothing our fight-or-flight response enables us to reduce the wear and tear on our bodies, feel more in control, and make better decisions. The success of the Stress Free program in reducing or managing stress is based on how effective it is at breaking Type 2 stress into more manageable Type 1 stress increments. The LifeSkills we teach are proven stress management skills that, with practice, will have you functioning in your optimal performance zone.

In that zone, you experience enough stress to feel challenged, excited, and engaged with life, but you don't experience so much that you're physically, mentally, or emotionally exhausted or overwhelmed. Think of this zone as a place where you're victorious over, rather than victimized by, the challenges you face in life. Be assured that the LifeSkills we'll show you will help you develop and function in this zone.

Below is a diagram that illustrates your optimal performance zone in relationship to the stress models we showed you earlier in this section:

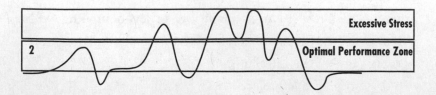

Learning to develop your optimal performance zone is deceptively simple. All you need to do is break up the destructive, cumulative negative effects of Type 2 stress into more manageable, short-term, even pleasurable Type 1 experiences. Doing this is simpler than you think. Teaching you how is the purpose of this book.

Each one of you has at least one physical or psychological response to stress that tells you you're facing a difficult situation. It can be tight muscles, a spasm, an eye twitch, a dry mouth, cold or clammy hands, sweating, or irritability. This is your signal that Type 2 stress is beginning to have a negative effect on your health, mood, and performance. As soon as you recognize this yellow, flashing caution light, it's time to implement one of the LifeSkills that you will learn in the following pages. Through practice, you can learn to leave the stress response behind and enter your optimal performance zone at will.

When you practice the LifeSkills, your heart rate, blood pressure, and breathing rate will drop to normal (or even a bit below normal, to compensate for the previous stress). Each time you practice a LifeSkill, the blood that left the thinking part of your brain starts to return. In just a few seconds of practice, you can bounce back free of the damage that would have occurred. Then you can continue whatever you were doing—working, driving, parenting, or even arguing with your lover—until the next caution light comes and you again practice one of the LifeSkills.

With repeated practice of these skills, you will spend more time in a state where you're mentally alert and physically relaxed. You will spend more time able to deal with your pressures and challenges. In that optimal performance zone, you will perform, think, and react your best, with few (or none) of the toxic effects of Type 2 stress.

Here's an example of how we taught workers in a company to use the Stress Free program to improve their health and productivity. This company had a high rate of employees with either muscular and/or carpal tunnel pain, as well as numerous disciplinary cases and union complaints. When we saw the bill processing department, we were appalled. Workers sat at terminals where billing envelopes from customers rapidly entered a slot and were slit open. In a matter of seconds, a worker had to determine if the check was enclosed, if it was made out in the right amount and was signed, if it had been sent in on time, if there were any past-due charges, and a whole host of other split-second decisions. Within a few more seconds, another bill entered the slot for processing. This repetitive process went on for *hours*.

A situation could not have been better designed to produce Type 2 stress—or to allow for study of such stress. Our research consisted of having a randomly selected group of workers learn one of the LifeSkills and then be allowed to interrupt the flow of the envelopes whenever they wanted to use this skill to alleviate their stress. What we discovered was that even though the workers could stop their bill-processing machines at any time, they actually took fewer unscheduled breaks and processed more bills accurately. Best of all, they did so with virtually no stress symptoms. These workers learned a specific LifeSkill that allowed them to voluntarily relax. As a result, they operated in their individual optimal performance zone throughout the day and had better health and less fatigue. The company reported better, more accurate performance, fewer disability claims, and fewer union complaints.

We have applied that same procedure in helping other workers maintain their optimal performance zone—accountants during tax season, airline pilots in the cramped quarters of a flight deck, air traffic controllers at major airports, and professional athletes seeking improved performance. In every instance, the approach was the same: each group of workers learned a LifeSkill and then was given the authority to use it when they felt they needed it. In each group, their performance improved, their fatigue decreased, and their health improved. In turn, their employers saw more accurate performance, greater productivity, and fewer disability claims.

Each of you will have the opportunity to use the LifeSkills to make a positive difference in your lives. You can practice one LifeSkill with your family when things get heated; you can practice another LifeSkill at work when things get chaotic; you can use still another LifeSkill when visiting the doctor or when your plane is gathering speed prior to takeoff. You will find that as you enter your optimal performance zone more readily, fewer situations will trigger your fight-or-flight response. You will find that in time your stress response will get triggered only in the sort of situations for which it was designed—that is, when you need the tension and sense of urgency to keep you safe from danger. In other situations you will remain focused and alert, able to deal successfully with the challenges you face.

In the next ten chapters, we offer and teach one LifeSkill per chapter. Each chapter begins with an explanation of the LifeSkill, a description of its value, and a sampling of the research that supports its selection. Each chapter includes stories of people with whom we have worked—people who now use the LifeSkills successfully in either their work or their home lives (or both). Finally, each chapter concludes with a step-by-step instructional guide to teach you exactly how to learn and practice the LifeSkill being presented.

CHAPTER 3

Breathe from Your Belly

Maddy came to the clinic because she was exhausted. She woke up every day tired and went to sleep tired. She was even tired of being tired! Besides tired, Maddy also felt stressed and overworked. She liked all the pieces of her life, but the whole was too much. In addition to working about fifty hours a week in a job she loved, Maddy had two children, a dog, and a husband she rarely saw. She was forty-one years old but complained that she felt sixty. From an objective point of view, her life worked. She was successful at work, had two lovely children, and had sustained a good marriage for seventeen years. Her husband loved her and she loved him.

Unfortunately, from Maddy's perspective, her life was far from successful. The stress and fatigue that she felt most of the time made it nearly impossible for her to appreciate her family and accomplishments. While her life looked good from the outside, on the inside it felt hollow and empty.

After numerous visits to her family doctor and a number of costly medical tests, Maddy was diagnosed with chronic fatigue syndrome. Chronic fatigue was more of a description of her condition than a diagnosis, reflecting the fact that the doctor could find no natural cause for her incessant fatigue. The diagnosis offered little solace to Maddy, who still felt miserable.

Maddy was an obviously attractive, intelligent, and good-natured woman. At first glance no one would imagine the strain she was under or how overwhelmed she felt. She spoke clearly and was cooperative and insightful. She had a good sense of humor and laughed when we told jokes. However, it didn't take long for us to see and hear that something was wrong with this picture. Maddy repeated the word *tired* over and over, and she conveyed an almost palpable sense that her life was missing something. "I know I should be happier than I am," she said. "Can you help me?"

From the beginning of our time with Maddy, we were struck by the simple observation that her breathing was too shallow. It was not getting sufficient oxygen into her brain and body, and therefore her nervous system was constantly over-loaded. Her current breathing pattern was, in effect, depriving her of oxygen; she was suffocating.

Instead of breathing slowly and deeply, Maddy took small breaths that barely ruffled her diaphragm. Unable to provide the energy required for the hundreds of thousands of chemical reactions her body conducted, Maddy's breathing was rapid and without the necessary depth. Her breathing mirrored the sense of unease she expressed. Our diagnosis was quick: we knew immediately that Maddy needed to practice the first

LifeSkill, belly-breathing. This is the simplest and most important LifeSkill. *Simple* because all we have to do is learn to breathe the way our bodies were designed, and *important* because the way we breathe is central to how much stress we experience.

We taught Maddy to slow down her breathing. We showed her how to focus her attention on her belly as she breathed in and out. We made sure her belly rose when she inhaled and fell when she exhaled. We guided her in practice of the amazing stress management properties of belly-breathing, and we watched her life change. Remarkably, within a few days Maddy was no longer constantly exhausted. She was tangibly enjoying her beautiful children and coming home at five on the dot because of her increased productivity at work. All in all, we had spent less than an hour with Maddy. It took maybe ten minutes of instruction and guided practice for her to learn belly-breathing, and that instructional session was followed by only one other visit to the clinic.

In addition to Maddy, we have worked with many other people who have been helped by belly-breathing. Jack, for example, was struggling with sciatica. Following a bicycle accident, he had pain that radiated from his buttocks and down into his leg for almost nine months. He was often grumpy and felt sorry for himself. Jack was forty-seven at the time of the accident and had been healthy his whole life. He was unprepared for the rigors of a body that no longer obeyed his every command. His physician told him there was nothing that could

be done. He was not a candidate for surgery, and his chiroprac-
tor gave him only temporary relief. He was referred to our
clinic because he was driving his wife crazy. She thought he
obsessed over his back and exaggerated the discomfort he felt.

Cathy, another patient of ours, struggled with the dual
responsibilities of completing her college degree while raising
a family. She had difficulty staying awake at night to study and
didn't like how she felt when she drank too much coffee.
Cathy needed to receive her teaching credential quickly,
because her husband's business was going through hard times.
They needed the income and health insurance that a teaching
job would provide. She, like Maddy, felt she was rushing
through her life and wondered why she wasn't having any fun.

We taught both Cathy and Jack the simple art of proper
breathing. We watched as their stress lessened and their
sense of efficacy improved. Through belly-breathing, Jack
was able to calm down and put his discomfort into perspective, thereby lessening the strain he put on his nervous system. As a result, his pain felt less intense. Cathy, like
Maddy, made better use of her time, and, like Jack, was able
to put her struggle into perspective. We have seen the profound effects of this simple practice over and over. After
teaching it to thousands of people, we're certain that this
essential LifeSkill is a key component for managing stress
and improving emotional competence. Now we want to
teach it to you.

At this point, some of you may be wondering why learning to breathe properly is so important. What is it about slow and deep breathing that's restorative? Why do we say this essential LifeSkill will reduce stress and improve well-being, as it did for Maddy, Jack, and Cathy? The answer is contained in the way the autonomic nervous system functions.

The autonomic nervous system is that part of your nervous system that controls basic life processes such as the rate of your heartbeat and the number of respirations you take. Until recently the autonomic nervous system was considered to operate entirely outside the scope of human control. Even scientists didn't think you could voluntarily slow your heartbeat or change the rate of digestion in your stomach. We now know this to be inaccurate. Many aspects of the autonomic nervous system *are* controllable, and breathing from the belly is the primary tool we have for regulating that system.

Actually, the very act of breathing is unique in the human body, since it's both automatic (in that we don't have to think about breathing) and voluntary (in the sense that we can decide to hold our breath). It's this juncture between the autonomic and voluntary nervous systems that makes belly-breathing such a powerful LifeSkill.

The autonomic nervous system is composed of two parts: the sympathetic and the parasympathetic branches. The sympathetic branch activates to help us deal with stress and is the part of the autonomic nervous system that initiates the fight-or-flight response. This sympathetic branch of the nervous system is what's responsible for the reactions we discussed in

Chapter 2. Our sympathetic nervous system gears us up to respond to danger and deal aggressively with life's challenges. Unfortunately, the sympathetic nervous system speaks only one language: red alert. It's good at responding but all too often incapable of shutting itself off. Turning off after the stress is over is the job of the other branch of the autonomic nervous system, the parasympathetic.

Generally speaking, the parasympathetic nervous system is that part of our nervous system that relaxes us. It gives us the ability to unwind and appreciate the beauty of a sunset. It allows our body to calm down after becoming stressed. It also helps us finally relax after a close call while driving. Were it not for the parasympathetic system, we would be unable to sit quietly and marvel at our children or relax enough to enjoy a symphony in the park.

The parasympathetic nervous system is marked by slow, regular, abdominal deep breathing. When your breathing is slow and deep, you feel relaxed. When your breathing is fast and shallow—as it is when the sympathetic nervous system is on red alert in response to real or perceived danger—you feel stressed. Now, if you're in real and imminent danger, you won't be able to take slow and regular deep breaths no matter how hard you try. And that's a good thing: if you're looking a tiger in the eye, and that tiger isn't behind bars in a zoo, the response of your sympathetic nervous system will help save you. In all other situations, though—for example, facing such "dangers" as an angry boss or an overloaded schedule—you

can voluntarily activate the parasympathetic system by breathing in a slow and deliberate manner into and out of your belly.
When you do this, you calm down your body. Since your mind
and body are in constant communication, a calm body will
give your mind a break.

Increased depth and decreased rate of breathing are the
best signs for your body to recognize that a threat has passed
and the rest of the body can calm down. In other words, the
rate and depth of your breathing are a link between the sympathetic and parasympathetic systems. That's why the simplest and most direct form of stress management is to change
your shallow, stressed breathing into belly-breathing. The
good news is that the simple act of slow, deep, and regular
breathing is a readily available tool.

And there's more good news: the proper regulation of the
sympathetic and parasympathetic nervous systems is the gateway into our optimal performance zone. On a practical level,
this means that whenever we experience Type 2 stress, we
have an effective tool for dealing with it. We can choose to
breathe slowly and deeply and enter the optimal performance
zone. When we choose to belly-breathe, we shut down the
stress response and save wear and tear on our nervous system
and heart. For Maddy and Cathy, the effects of stress included
being tired and feeling overwhelmed. The change that belly-
breathing had on them was profound. They learned that they
could recognize which part of their nervous system was active
and, when the sympathetic system was in overdrive, could

access the "control switch" that gave them the power to turn it off. This newfound ability had positive effects in all areas of their lives.

Your stress response starts almost immediately when you perceive danger. You're ready to face that danger within the first heartbeat of seeing it. The problem is that you're also geared up to face danger within one heartbeat of remembering the deadline at work or the amount of work you have to do. The instant reaction exists because your body can't wait a second if a tiger is really chasing you. You've got to do something *immediately* to save yourself. Our bodies, designed for self-preservation, have a built-in safeguard to make sure that physical response doesn't relax until the coast is really clear. That's why you have to practice belly-breathing for between six and ten seconds—until the all clear is sounded.

However, with six to ten seconds of regular practice, even Jack learned to take a break from stress. Poor Jack: every time his back hurt his mind went into overdrive. "What if I never play tennis again?" "What if I can't even roll on the floor when I have grandchildren?" "What if my back *always* hurts?" "What happens if it gets worse?" Jack literally drove himself (and his wife) crazy with his worrying. His practice of belly-breathing allowed first his body to get a break, and then his mind. Jack, being the trouper he is, took to this LifeSkill with a vengeance. He practiced all the time and discovered the absence of stress at the end of the rainbow.

What Jack found was that when he practiced belly-breathing regularly, he became more relaxed. He didn't just calm down more efficiently from stress; he actually became more peaceful. After a couple of weeks of practice, his nervous system began to change, and he found himself calmer more often, less tired, and more optimistic. The point at which stress began to affect him rose, and fewer things ruffled his equilibrium. As he became more peaceful, his flight-or-flight response was triggered less often by false alarms, saving itself for when it was really needed. With fewer stress chemicals coursing through his body, his perception of pain changed and he was able to endure the occasional pain he had. Fewer stress chemicals meant he responded with panic less often and was able to put his disability in perspective. He saw things a lot more clearly and was able to develop the patience it took for his back to finally heal.

Like Jack, Cathy, and Maddy, you too will benefit from belly-breathing. And you can begin at this very moment. Learning to breathe fully and deeply may be the single greatest gift you can give your body and your mind. Not only does belly-breathing reduce stress chemicals and muscle tension, but it also allows your body to relax enough for positive emotions such as happiness to appear. The goal of the Stress Free program is a life of contentment, health, and happiness. Learning to breathe slowly, fully, and deeply is the cornerstone LifeSkill. For almost all people we have worked with, belly-breathing on its own is enough to both reduce stress and increase happiness.

LifeSkill Exercise:
Breathe from Your Belly

Purpose

The purpose of this LifeSkill is . . .

- To teach you the simplest form of stress management.
- To remind you that you have a remarkable body that can be taught to relax.
- To help you balance your nervous system.
- To show you that belly-breathing helps you think in more productive ways.

Practice

1. As you inhale, imagine that your belly is a big balloon that you're slowly filling with air.
2. Place your hands on your belly while you slowly inhale.
3. Watch your hands as they rise with your in-breath.
4. Watch your hands fall as you slowly breathe out, letting the air out of the balloon.
5. As you exhale, make sure your belly stays relaxed.
6. Take at least two or three more slow and deep breaths, making sure to keep your attention on the rise and fall of your belly.

Tips

- Make sure you practice every single day.
- Sometimes practice for five to ten minutes at a time.
- You can practice even when you're not under stress—for example, while you're sitting in your car, watching TV, walking for exercise, or sitting at the computer at work.

Application

Use this LifeSkill . . .

- When you feel angry.
- Before getting on an airplane if you're nervous.
- When you need to pause and think before speaking, to avoid saying something you might later regret.
- When you need help falling asleep.
- Whenever you notice that your breathing is shallow, rapid, tight, or tense.

"BREATHE FROM YOUR BELLY" LIFESKILL:

Breathing slowly and deeply into and out of your belly is a signal to your mind and body to let go of stress and improve your health and happiness.

CHAPTER 4

So Much to Appreciate

Stress is everywhere. We struggle with demands at work, demands at home, illness, traffic, crying babies, annoying bosses, and other assorted irritations. Hassles are everywhere, and we need skills to cope. In fact, there's an entire area of stress research devoted to hassles such as not being able to find the car keys or dealing with a rude sales clerk. According to Dr. Richard Lazarus of the University of California at Berkeley, these little hassles really add up over the course of a day or week. Although not catastrophic, like a serious accident or illness, these minor life hassles have a cumulative effect and can lead to mistakes at work, or even to illness.

Fortunately, the first LifeSkill, belly-breathing, is an antidote to both large and small hassles. Doing belly-breathing lowers your blood pressure, relaxes your muscles, and helps you manage your emotions. Belly-breathing creates peace in your mind as well as your body. We know that, with practice, you will see positive results. Belly-breathing is the foundation of the Stress Free program.

Now, in this chapter, we introduce you to the second LifeSkill. Practice of this new skill offers immediate help with stress and allows the opportunity to feel joy and happiness. This skill, the art of appreciation, will do as much as belly-breathing to improve your life.

Appreciation is the simple act of noticing the good in your life. It means seeing the love represented by family and friends. It means being grateful for the bounty of monetary success, not taking for granted the routine material blessings of home, car, and food. It means really seeing your beautiful surroundings. It means being able to notice the good in each remarkable day. It means being able to marvel at the simple things our bodies do, such as moving, eating and sitting. It means being able to really appreciate the smile of a small child and the profound gift of lifetime friendship.

Learning to see the simple blessings sounds easy, but for most of us it's much harder than one would think. We become overwhelmed by our struggles and stress and lose sight of how much we have to be thankful for. The obvious reason is that it's easy to notice the ways in which our lives are difficult, but it takes effort to see the good. Our stress announces itself loudly and with great fanfare; we can't miss an illness or a broken car or a difficulty with a neighbor or friend. But we can (and do) easily miss the routine, yet wonderful, aspects of our life.

George could describe every detail of the pressure he felt at work and the way his demanding boss talked to him. Elaine painted a picture of all of the struggles that faced her and her family. She single-handedly cared for her sick mother as well as her children, because her husband traveled much of the time. Jill was eminently clear about the difficulty of living with a chronic illness. With her symptoms at the tip of her tongue, she talked easily of her fatigue and frustration.

Each of these individuals had legitimate stresses and suffered because of them. We sympathized with each and every person and understood that each situation was difficult. However, we could see that these people also suffered because of something else—something that intensified the stress: they suffered because they had lost sight of the good things that were in their lives. They had stopped counting their blessings and started to see their cups as half empty rather than half full. They found it difficult to remember the beauty in their lives, and the failure to do so intensified the toll stress exacted.

Jill was a thirty-eight-year-old woman with chronic diabetes and a busy and full life. Her diabetes wasn't entirely controlled by the combination of medication, exercise, and diet. If she exercised every day and was perfect in what she ate, her illness was manageable. But who (she would ask herself, after skipping a day of exercise or eating more calories than she should) could live like that? Jill hated the fatigue and lightheadedness she experienced, the dietary restrictions she faced, and the necessity of regular exercise. In short, managing her illness had turned Jill into a frustrated and unhappy woman.

George worked for a start-up in Silicon Valley that began after the stock market bubble burst. He worked long hours and under a lot of pressure. He arrived at the office early in the morning and stayed late each evening. George remained with this job because he had the opportunity to make a lot of money and he liked the challenge of seeing if he could usher this company to success.

For a while his job was only demanding, difficult, and tiring. What put George over the edge was the arrival of Tom, his new manager. Tom was an exacting and critical perfectionist, always in a hurry, and a poor communicator. Each of these traits drove George nuts. He said to himself almost every day, "This damn job is tough enough without Tom making it worse. I just can't stand him." Working for this company led George to develop high blood pressure and tension headaches. On a normal day he would feel the muscles in his back and neck tighten just as soon as he went into work.

When George saw Tom coming toward him with that telltale critical look on his face, it was hard not to scream at Tom to leave him alone. George had to bite his tongue ten times a day, and exercising such self-control took energy from George that he didn't have. To make matters worse, George had trouble sleeping and argued constantly with his wife. The bottom line for George, as it was for Jill, was that life had ceased to be fun. Their problems loomed so large that they metaphorically blotted out the sun.

We see a great many people who look and sound like

George, Jill, and Elaine. Stress makes them lose sight of what's good, and that partial blindness makes them suffer more. A recent study of working women showed that the most pressing everyday problem they faced was stress. A recent study by Dr. Ron Z. Goetzel, director of research at Medstat, evaluated over 100,000 employees of Citibank. He found that too much stress was more likely to make people ill and disabled than familiar high-risk behaviors such as smoking, being overweight, and having high blood pressure.

Too many people we see are so used to being stressed that they find it hard to relax enough to smell the roses. What they don't understand is that this inability to smell the roses is part of their body's response to stress. Not only does stress reduce their happiness minute to minute, but it makes it harder to relax over the long haul. Stress does its damage not just when it happens but over the course of a day or week. The hatred that George felt for his boss carried over to simple, unrelated tasks such as taking out the garbage and cleaning out his car.

An unrelenting stress response ensures that your body won't let you appreciate a sunset or the smile of your baby. Remember, Type 2 stress makes you feel as if you're in danger all the time. This sense of danger, which makes you narrowly focus your attention, is the opposite of the relaxed feeling you need to enjoy your life. The huge cost of this type of stress is that you have a difficult time letting go. The overstimulation of the stress response makes frustration, tight shoulders, and a grouchy mood the status quo. This help explains why you notice your struggles easily and find it hard to appreciate the good stuff.

The practice of appreciation reverses this trend. It teaches you to treasure the good and spend time thinking about your blessings. Appreciation takes advantage of our parasympathetic nervous system to reduce the stress response and trigger our optimal performance zone. Looking for things to appreciate reduces stress and actually retrains our nervous system to make it easier to relax. Here are the reasons.

We've told you how stress triggers the sympathetic nervous system: when you see your boss coming at you with more work, or when your ex tells you he or she can't take the kids again this weekend, your mind communicates to your body that you're in danger. While the danger isn't an oncoming car or advancing tiger, it's a danger to your well-being nonetheless. Anytime your thoughts or images bring up danger via an ex-spouse, a boss, or a misbehaving child, your body releases stress chemicals to help you face the problem.

We've described to you the damage this overuse of the stress response causes to your body and mind. The good news is that your body can be taught to respond differently. When you learn to notice the good things that surround you and think positive, loving thoughts, you can reverse the stress response, stopping it in its tracks and beginning a healing process. Since your nervous system is set up to make sure that you're safe, it makes sense to gear up to fight when your boss relentlessly comes at you with more and more work. However, your nervous system is also there to help you appreciate the beautiful things in your life, if you would only let it. If you spend a few moments thinking lovingly of your family, for example, you can engage the parasympathetic nervous system, and it will calm your mind and body.

When your mind brings up pictures of a rotten boss, huge piles of work, an unkind spouse, and endless problems, what else can your body do but get tight? Those pictures are signals to your brain and body that something is not okay and you need to be prepared for danger. They're tools that your own self is using to keep you safe and alive, signs that your nervous system is doing a good job of keeping you alert to danger. Yet the same stress response that helps you combat danger and frustration can prevent you from truly experiencing the joys of life. The stress response simply ignores all the good aspects of life that have nothing to do with danger or problems; they're irrelevant in the urgency of danger. And yet love, care, beauty, family, nature, and kindness trigger a response of their own.

What is that response? How does the nervous system react to positive images? What happens inside when you think appreciative and loving thoughts? It's nothing like the stress response, because when you experience love and care and appreciation, your body recognizes that it has nothing to defend itself against. What is there to fight with or protect from? To make sure you don't feel too much love or see too much beauty? When you have thoughts of good things, when your mind pictures loving scenes, your body has no need for tension and high blood pressure. In fact, loving thoughts and the emotion of gratitude are as good for the body as a relaxing massage on the beach in Hawaii.

Your mind and body can fully relax in four to six beats of your heart, or around six seconds, when you bring to your mind's eye a beautiful sunset, a friend's kindness, or the special joy of a loving spouse. When you pay attention to these positive things, you're sending your body the message that life is good and it can relax. Many good things happen to your body when you count your blessings. All the harmful changes that take place when you're under stress reverse when you think loving and appreciative thoughts. The simple shifting of attention from problems to appreciation lowers your stress as effectively as anything else you can do.

For example . . .

- Stress lowers the effectiveness of your immune system. In contrast, thinking of someone you really care about gives your immune system a boost.
- Stress makes your blood pressure rise. Thinking fondly of a loved one you're about to see lowers your blood pressure.
- Stress causes your heart rate to rise and your stomach to churn. Remembering a kindness done to you lowers your heart rate and calms your stomach.

- Stress causes your thinking to become narrow and focused on the problem. Remembering how much you appreciate the way your dog runs after a ball makes your mind more creative.
- Rehashing an old argument triggers the fight-or-flight response. Rehashing a day spent with a lover shuts down fight-or-flight in about six seconds.

A number of years ago, Dr. David McClelland demonstrated the benefits of such positive thoughts in what he termed the "Mother Teresa effect." He showed a group of students a film about Mother Teresa caring for sick and impoverished people in the slums of India. After viewing the film, the students showed an increase in the functioning of their immune system.

When you see goodness or think positive thoughts, the message sent to your body is that life is good. Except in the rare instances when you're truly in danger, this is the message you want your body to have. If a tiger is really coming at you or a car is bearing down on you, you won't be able (and won't want) to think of a beautiful sunset for four heartbeats. You will immediately and almost unconsciously do everything possible to get yourself out of danger. However, if after surviving a close call in your car you then mentally replay the danger over and over, or tell twenty people about the incident, you will cause additional, unnecessary stress. If instead you think about how lucky you are to see your children again, that positive emotion will quickly soothe your tension and anxiety.

The power of appreciation is as simple and profound as belly-breathing. A small amount of this practice goes a long way. When we first talked with George, he wanted to rant and rave about his boss for our entire session. Instead, after only a few minutes, we asked him to tell us about his family. It was clear from his response that he loved his wife and children and hated how his exhaustion and stress affected them. All we had to do was ask him how he felt when thinking of his son fast asleep in his lap to bring a smile to his face. "My family isn't the problem," he told us. We said, "We know that, but they can be the solution."

One of George's complaints was he hated his job so much that he resented waking up to his alarm clock. During the practice of this LifeSkill, he had an appreciation break-through. He realized that he was fortunate to have a job that allowed him to support himself and his family. With that insight, and the practice of remembering that "aha" realization every day, George shifted his point of view. It now includes thankfulness for the alarm clock that wakes him for the job that supports his family.

Jill wanted to tell us how uncomfortable she was and how hard it is to manage diabetes. We listened, acknowledged her struggle, and even agreed with her. Then we wondered aloud how her life would have been if she'd suffered from the same disease only sixty years earlier, before easily administered oral medication and before the simple finger-resting of blood sugar levels. She grudgingly acknowledged those advances and even brought up how lucky she was to have a health facility at work. Jill was then asked which experience was more pleasant, thinking of her problems or stopping for a moment to count her blessings. We also asked her to reflect on her ability to think clearly. She responded unequivocally that appreciation felt better and offered a much-needed rest from the anxiety-ridden, panicky thinking she was accustomed to. She quickly grasped that much of her suffering stemmed from simply not seeing the forest for the trees.

Now the question emerges: How do you develop and practice appreciation? The answer is simple. Learn to focus your attention on things that are beautiful, times when you've felt love in your heart, instances of gratitude for the kindness people have done for you. Learn to see the good in life as readily as you see the bad; learn to see beauty as readily as you see ugliness; and in particular learn to see kindness as readily as you see unkindness.

We gave a simple practice to Lois, an emergency room nurse. She worked in a high-stress environment and struggled to find beauty in a world of suffering. Lois loved nature and spoke with special fondness of the grace and freedom of birds flying effortlessly overhead. In our session, we asked her to focus her attention completely on the mental image of a colorful bird. She was to look in awe as she imagined the movement of its wings, heard the sounds as it passed, and pictured the incredible color of the sky above. In other words, for fifteen seconds or so she was to really pay attention and "appreciate" the beauty of this common scene in nature.

As Lois was visualizing the bird, we suggested that she try to feel the loveliness of the scene in her body. Many people experience beauty and love as warmth in the area around their heart. Other people just feel at peace. Lois was one of the latter. We asked her to take a mental snapshot of her body as it was at peace. We asked her to store the feeling as a memory that she could access during stressful times in her day. We left her with the exhortation to appreciate beauty and goodness often. We found, with Lois and many others, that appreciation became a positive addiction, something they couldn't do without and that made their days richer, fuller, and healthier.

LifeSkill Exercise:
So Much to Appreciate

Purpose

The purpose of this LifeSkill is . . .

- To help you acknowledge the good in your life, which will give you a warm feeling inside.
- To help you feel more peaceful and less stressed.
- To improve your relationships.

Practice

Before you begin your day's activities:

1. Review the things you need to get done during the day.
2. Include on your list two specific things to be thankful for.

During a stressful time:

1. Take two slow, deep belly-breaths.
2. When inhaling for your third breath, think deeply on one of the following: someone you love, a beautiful place, an act of kindness done for you.

During the day:

1. For fifteen to thirty seconds focus your full attention on someone you love.
2. For fifteen to thirty seconds appreciate a place you find beautiful.
3. For fifteen to thirty seconds think fondly about a kindness someone did for you.

Tips

- When you think about a person you love, think of someone with whom you're still in a good relationship.
- When you think of a place, think about a place that evokes good memories or is particularly beautiful.
- When you think about a kind act, think clearly about what someone did that was loving.
- Appreciating positive things is enhanced when combined with belly-breathing.

Application

Use this LifeSkill . . .

- When stress and difficulties pile up.
- When there's just too much to do.
- When you have to make a decision.
- Before making a difficult phone call.
- When you feel unappreciated.

- When talking with a family member, lover, or friend, to remember how much that person means to you.
- When feeling lonely or isolated.

"SO MUCH TO APPRECIATE" LIFESKILL:

Appreciating other people, the beauty of nature, and the joys of everyday life may be the simplest and most immediate way to create both health and happiness.

CHAPTER 5

Tense to Relax

Joann noticed that every single time she had any contact with her ex-husband she felt sick afterward. Her muscles felt tight and her stomach felt queasy. This was quite a problem, because she saw Jack at least twice every week. Joann and Jack shared custody of their two children and regularly transported them from home to home. Joann started to dread Friday and Sunday evenings because of the effect that seeing Jack had on her. She complained constantly to her friends that it was Jack's fault because of how he treated her, but this didn't help prevent the negative response she felt. Even three years after the divorce, Joann felt connected in the worst way to someone she wanted to be done with.

Kathy had a similar problem, except that it was her boss who continually caused her stress. A secretary in a large corporation, Kathy had recently been reassigned. Her old boss had retired—a man with whom she had worked for years and who felt like family. Her new boss, Gloria, was all work, and Kathy didn't like the atmosphere one bit. Gloria expected all of her people to work exceptionally hard, and that meant little chitchat and long, intense workdays. Kathy resented Gloria's approach and missed the friendliness and warmth she had shared with her colleagues in the past. When we first saw Kathy, she reported that she was stressed out of her mind. To her it was torture just to get off the freeway and go to work. Simply picturing Gloria's face was enough to cause Kathy's jaw to clench and her breathing to become shallow and forced.

Both Kathy and Joann were in the midst of difficult life situations. It isn't easy to co-parent with someone you've divorced, nor is it easy to adapt to an especially demanding boss. Both Kathy and Joann, adjusting poorly to their circumstances, were drowning in stress. The first thing we noticed with both women was how tight their bodies looked. From their stiff faces to their tight posture and tense movements, both women appeared frustrated, angry, ill at ease, easily distracted, and troubled. They were living testaments to the power stress has to create muscle tightness and strain.

Tight muscles, clenched fists, and a constantly upset stomach are indications that stress has a hold on your emotional and physical well-being. And yet the damage stress causes goes further than these symptoms. Kathy and Joann were so stressed they literally forgot how to relax. Their bodies had started to take tight muscles and a racing heart as normal. When we asked Kathy and Joann what they did to relax, they laughed and said, "Relax? You've got to be kidding." Because of the stress they were under, they'd almost forgotten how to let go.

Their bodies had gotten so used to feeling tense that Kathy and Joann could no longer feel relaxed, even when doing things they enjoyed. This inability to remember feeling peaceful causes people like them to lose hope and perspective—not to mention sleep. It was time for them to learn a simple yet powerful skill that enables relaxation even when stress is high and relief feels far away.

Sometimes our minds are so agitated that we can't think straight and we feel trapped. Kathy certainly fit into this category. She was so upset over the way her new boss treated her, and so lost without her old boss, that just showing up at work made her anxious and uncomfortable. She considered an aching back and neck normal and saw the twitches she was developing as inevitable. We told her emphatically that body pain is *not* normal and that muscle twitching is *not* the only (and certainly not the best) way to handle difficult challenges at work. But since Kathy's mind was agitated just thinking about work, we figured she would need to relax her body before taking on new insights with her mind.

We taught both Kathy and Joann the LifeSkill of tensing up in order to relax, and both showed marked improvement in a short period of time. They were able to relax their bodies and then their minds with short periods of daily practice. This particular LifeSkill was chosen for these women because it focuses first on quieting the activity of the body. For Kathy and Joann, attempting to quiet and focus their minds was possible only when they were able to get their bodies into a comfortable state.

As you know from our discussion of the stress response in Chapter 2, our muscles become tight and blood flow to the hands and feet becomes restricted under stress. The exciting news is that we can teach you to instruct your body to have the opposite, relaxed response so that you can recover quickly from the stress of an ex-husband or a difficult boss. When your muscles are tense and contracted, they feel light. By contrast, when your muscles are relaxed, they feel heavy. Remember how heavy and soft a sleeping baby or child feels? Compare lifting a relaxed infant to touching someone who is angry or anxious. There's nothing soft about *that*.

One of the interesting things about the muscles in the human body is that they relax to their utmost right after they've been tensed. Try it right now: clench your fist for a few seconds and then completely relax your hand. You will see that your hand goes from feeling light to feeling heavy. This is because muscles relax the most after they've been tensed or contracted. Tensing and relaxing is a skill so simple that you can practice by gripping and releasing the steering wheel of your car at a stoplight or in traffic jam. Whenever you practice, you will notice how quickly the shift from muscle tension to muscle relaxation happens.

We have mentioned over and over that LifeSkills need to be *practiced*. Once you've learned and practiced each skill, the relaxation you get will be almost instantaneous. You can relax your body in less than ten seconds and free your mind in the same amount of time. It's as simple as watching your hand relax after you've made a fist. Your whole body can relax that quickly.

The first thing that happened to Kathy through the use of this LifeSkill was that she realized how tense she was when she felt normal. She couldn't believe how much tension she had been under! Next, she realized that if she could consciously relax her body at least for a moment, she could do so for longer periods of time. This was exciting news for Kathy, and she practiced every chance she got. It didn't take too long before she could in fact relax her body for not seconds but minutes—and then more. Finally, Kathy realized that as her body relaxed, her mind slowed down, allowing her thought processes to clear up.

Lots of folks are like Joann and Kathy, needing to relax their bodies to make relaxing their minds possible. Fortunately, the mind and body are so closely linked that relaxing one will relax the other. Kathy and Joann (and thousands of other people) will tell you that your mind will follow your relaxed body into a state of quiet. By tensing and relaxing the muscles of your body, you not only overcome the physical tension caused by stress, you also begin to quiet your mind. Joanne learned through practice of this LifeSkill that she could see her ex-husband without feeling exhausted. Her headaches decreased in frequency and intensity, and she no longer needed to take two Advil every time she saw Jack.

The idea behind tensing to relax is based on the research of a physician named Dr. Edmund Jacobson. He discovered that people could activate specific muscles just by imagining doing an activity. He placed electrodes on the body to measure muscle activity while people imagined performing various activities. He found that when people imagined they were walking, for example, the electrodes measured activity in the actual muscles used for walking. When he had people imagine they were eating, their jaw muscles became more active, though there was no obvious chewing motion. Dr. Jacobson concluded that many medical problems were the result of people creating muscle tension without being aware that they were doing so.

To help reduce the muscle tension, Dr. Jacobson developed a stress management training that focuses on tensing and relaxing specific muscles. Dr. Jacobson's approach achieved widespread recognition during WWII, when it was used by combat pilots to remain relaxed but alert while sitting in the confined cockpits of their fighter planes. Although tensing to relax may seem simple, there's a great deal of medical research showing that this skill can positively affect a great variety of stress-related conditions, including chronic pain, muscle strain, tension headache, back and neck pain, and dental problems such as grinding of one's teeth; enhance rehabilitation from stroke; and improve athletic performance ranging from running to golf.

Let's look at another example of how this LifeSkill helped

improve a significant medical problem In 2001, Jonathan was still riding high on the crest of the Silicon Valley computer boom. He was thirty-seven, which was considered old by many computer geniuses, and a senior vice-president with a major computer company. He had all the trappings of success, including a Porsche convertible, a very small (but hugely overpriced) multi-million-dollar house in the Bay Area, a condominium in Hawaii, and a cellar full of the most expensive Napa Valley wines. Up at the crack of dawn each day, Jonathan worked late into the night, using the phone and the Internet to troubleshoot computer installations in Europe in the morning and in Asia at night. It was not uncommon for him to get only four or five hours of sleep, but fatigue was a badge of honor and accomplishment among his peers.

On the downside, he was a chain smoker, had gained a good deal of weight, and enjoyed all the nutritional benefits of junk food at every meal (washed down with the best of wines). He had a nonstop caffeine buzz that helped him stay focused on his computer business but little else. And when the computer bubble suddenly burst, the stock options with which he financed his extravagant lifestyle plummeted in value. His modest house was now worth less than he bought it for (though the huge mortgage was very real), his job was in jeopardy, and if he was forced to join the ranks of the unemployed he would be competing with many other talented people looking for the same kind of employment. Most distressing of all was the fact that he had no friends in whom he could confide.

One night, working late in his office, he was all but alone in the building. Sitting at his desk, he experienced an odd pain in his left shoulder and neck. Assuming it was muscle strain from the hours he spent hunched over his keyboard, he ignored the early pain. Over the next few hours, however, this progressed to a stabbing pain in the back and then a sudden crushing pain in his chest that was unmistakably a heart attack. At that point he signaled the night security staff and was rushed to Stanford University Hospital, where he survived due to an emergency angioplasty.

When we saw him in an outpatient clinic two weeks later, Jonathan was scared. He had never thought of himself as being under too much stress, because a fast and furious pace was business as usual for him and his colleagues. Since the LifeSkill of tensing to relax is known to be very effective with cardiovascular problems, that's the one we first taught him. A reluctant student initially, he hated slowing down. In his high-speed Internet world, slowing down meant falling behind, being an underachiever, and being useless. It took Jonathan about four months to learn how to relax and yet remain mentally alert.

Jonathan's big challenge came just as he was finishing his cardiac rehabilitation program. He was offered a new position in a start-up computer company, and even thinking about returning to that pressured environment made him breathe shallowly and caused his blood pressure to rise. He was afraid that he would get right back into his old patterns and that next time he might suffer a fatal heart attack. Jonathan was rightfully scared. The good news is that he was scared enough to practice tensing to relax on a regular basis, even while he was at his desk at work.

To address Jonathan's fears we helped him design a slow transition back to work. We gave him practice guidelines, monitored his success, and saw him weekly during his transition. We also helped him design an *affirmation*, or positive coping statement, that he could repeat to himself. We often find it helpful to combine the physical relaxation of tensing and relaxing with the mental relaxation of saying something positive to oneself—a statement that generates peace and calm. Jonathan found tensing and relaxing easy, once he accepted the need to slow down, but struggled with the affirmation.

It took Jonathan a while, but he eventually developed an affirmation that helped him maintain a healthy and calm perspective on his life, even when he was at work. When things got intense at the office, Jonathan would first ask himself: "Is this worth dying for?" Inevitably and always the answer was no, and that negative would remind him to practice his affirmation: "I work hard and remain relaxed and focused." To this day (almost four years later) he still practices this LifeSkill and is doing well at work and in life.

Jonathan settled on a routine of practicing tensing to relax for a few minutes each morning, then a couple of times during the day, and again a couple of times every evening.

This practice moderated the stress that he was under and taught him he could work without killing himself. He was able to report that his new job and the stress of work did not lead to distress and illness.

Please don't think that Jonathan had only smooth sailing. It was rough going for a while, in life-threatening swells. However, with practice Jonathan developed the confidence that he could minimize the stress of his work—and developed the ability to do so. Interestingly, we found his question about stress and dying to be insightful and effective in our lives as well. We have asked ourselves and many of our patients, "Is this worth dying for?" Inevitably, for us as for Jonathan, the answer is a resounding no. Then we too take a deep breath, say something positive, and tense and relax our muscles.

LifeSkill Exercise:
Tense to Relax

Purpose

The purpose of this LifeSkill is . . .

- To experience the difference between muscle tension and relaxation.
- To relax deeply and fully.
- To teach your body to become stress free.

Practice

1. Take two slow, deep belly-breaths.
2. On the third inhalation, tighten your right arm from your shoulder to your hand.
3. Hold tightly for two or three seconds.
4. As you exhale, relax fully and let your arm drop.
5. Repeat the first four steps with your other arm, each leg, and then your entire body.
6. As you practice, repeat a relaxing affirmation, such as, "I have all the time in the world" or "I am relaxed and at peace."

Tips

- When you tense your muscles, really *tense* them; when you relax, really *relax*.
- When you inhale, fill up your belly with air.
- When you exhale, let your belly relax and stay soft.
- Remind yourself how calm and relaxed you are and remember that you're capable of this kind of relaxation at any time. Pay attention to what it feels like to be relaxed.
- Think often during your day, "I'm relaxed and at peace."
- Sometimes practice with only your arms or legs, and sometimes your entire body.

Application

Use this LifeSkill . . .

- Before going to bed.
- To feel alert when you awaken in the morning.
- Before physical exercise.
- When your neck and/or shoulders are tight.
- When you're sitting at your desk.
- When you're stuck in traffic.
- When you're sitting in an airplane.

"TENSE TO RELAX" LIFESKILL:

When you tense your muscles, letting go allows you to relax deeply.

CHAPTER 6

Visualize Success

Sam was stuck. He felt trapped and frustrated. He had been offered a promotion at work that involved moving to another city. It was a dream job, and yet Sam didn't know if he could make the life transition work. Sam's daughter was sixteen, a junior in high school, and she threatened to disown him if they moved. His wife was happy where they were too; however, she said she would give up the job she loved and move if it was what he really wanted. His son, at twelve, was at best ambivalent about leaving his middle school and his friends.

Sam wanted everyone to be happy, himself included. Making this big decision was driving him crazy, because he wanted to please everyone but couldn't figure out how. At one point he got so wound up about the whole process that he asked his dog what *he* wanted to do.

Sam agonized over this decision for weeks. His company, doing its best to be accommodating, made the situation worse by telling him there was no hurry to decide. The job was his for the taking, his boss said. Sam went back and forth between the demands of his career and the desires of his family. Every time he thought about what to do, he searched for an answer that would please everyone—and every time he failed. He began to get headaches when he mulled over the problem. Soon these became more frequent, and then they were accompanied by neck spasms and muscle tension. Sam's well-intentioned goal to please everyone was leading to nothing but frustration. He felt helpless and hopeless, convinced that he would never make the right decision.

When we saw Sam, he said he was going crazy over what he thought should be a simple decision. As he described the situation to us, we saw that the problem lay in his approach: each time he pushed himself to find the perfect solution and was unsuccessful, he perpetuated a vicious cycle. The stress he felt reduced his ability to problem-solve and think creatively. Sam's effort to do the right thing, a laudable goal in itself, became an impediment, and he and his family spent many an unhappy evening as a result.

After we saw Sam in the clinic, where he complained of headaches, back pain, and an upset stomach, his life began to change for the better. We helped Sam by teaching him about the power of his mind to visualize a successful outcome to his problem—that is, to picture that outcome in his mind. We reminded him of an important fact: that his body reacts to whatever he pictures in his mind. For example, his body would react to the fear of a nighttime intruder in his living room by tensing up. Likewise, his body would react to the sound of his cat rummaging around in the basement if he thought the cat was an intruder.

When Sam, like the rest of us, hears an unknown noise in the basement, his mind pictures an intruder. When he sees that intruder in his mind's eye, his body reacts as if there were a real intruder, not just a cat. We humans think not just in words but in sounds, pictures, and textures. These mental sounds, pictures, and textures are very powerful, and they can be used both to stress us out and to heal us from stress.

Here's the simple experiment we offered Sam. You can practice it too, to experience firsthand how imagery affects you physically. Imagine yourself in your kitchen, standing over a cutting board. You have in front of you a knife and a basket of delicious fruit. From that bowl, select a beautiful orange, fragrant and heavy with juice, and place it on the cutting board. Notice the brightness of its color and the familiar texture of its rind. Now slowly cut the orange in half, and then in quarters. Notice the difference in color and texture between the cut surfaces and the peel. In your mind, watch yourself pick up one piece and slowly raise it to your mouth. Notice how you anticipate the taste, how you're familiar with the fragrance. Now picture yourself biting into the orange to capture its sweetness.

Most people feel an actual release of saliva from the back of their cheeks when they do this. Even while reading this book, you can experience the sweetness of the orange, because you can draw on your body's memory and give your mind a powerful image of a pleasurable experience. This kind of positive imagery can be healing to your body and mind. Unfortunately, picturing a tasty orange—as Sam did when he tried our experiment—is different from seeing the stressful pictures that were running through Sam's head.

If visualizing a juicy orange for even a few seconds makes you salivate, think what would happen if you visualized yourself as stressed out for hours, days, weeks, and even months on end? These are the kind of images that Sam experienced. We're here to tell you that seeing negative images in your mind has a detrimental physical effect on your body. This effect occurs through the same pathways that allow your body to generate saliva when you imagine an orange.

If, like Sam, you focus again and again on a difficult situation, this conveys a powerful negative message to your nervous system, and all the muscles and organs of your body respond. One of the most basic responses to stress is for the muscles of the entire body to clench and become rigid so that you can remain upright for fighting or use that strength to run away. Since the muscles of the back are some of the largest and most powerful of the body, they're particularly sensitive. That's why back pain is a common response to stress. This connection between mind and body helps explain why negative images often become self-fulfilling prophecies: the negative images we have of ourselves have the power to create negative experiences in our bodies. Sam referred to the job decision and its resultant stress as "a pain in the neck"—and neck pain was one of the symptoms he displayed.

At first Sam ignored the muscle pain and headaches, taking aspirin with desperate regularity and simply forging ahead. As he continued to experience the pressure to decide, he started to see his employer and his family as burdens; they were forcing him to make the right decision. One phrase that he used over and over to describe his feelings to us was, "I just want them all to get off my back!" As he uttered those words after a couple of sessions with us, he finally realized that his mental image of carrying the burden of this decision for his family was manifesting itself as physical back pain.

As we worked with Sam, we pointed out that one reason he had such a hard time solving his job problem was that he constantly pictured himself failing. For example, he used his power of imagination to see his daughter hating him. Over and over again he heard the contempt in her voice as she said she would hate him forever if they moved. He pictured himself staying put, saw images of himself at his desk, staring off into space wondering where his career had gone. He had a particularly alarming picture of himself as an old man still struggling to make good decisions and blaming himself for the poor ones he had made. Sam was a good visualizer all right— a prime example of someone using *negative* images to make himself miserable. Our goal was to teach him to use the power of *positive* images of success to help himself.

Cyndi was another patient who needed to learn to visualize success. A single parent raising two children and sharing custody with her ex-husband, she was a working mother who felt crazed every morning and evening trying to get her chores and responsibilities done. She came into the clinic complaining of tension headaches. Like Sam, she created bleak pictures of her day. Her primary image was of a woman who was overworked, underloved, overtired, and harried. She described to us a woman who crawled into bed each evening exhausted and discouraged. She felt like a failure and pictured herself as one. We commented to her that she might as well put a big red F on her forehead.

Cyndi had no idea how to manage her stress, and she didn't realize how strongly her image of herself as a failure affected her body. She didn't understand, for example, that her image of herself as an unsupported and lonely woman was affecting her posture. Instead of standing upright, she stood with shoulders rounded and slumped, which put greater pressure on her back even when she was sitting. Even after we explained the workings of stress, she had a hard time believing that the way she saw herself was related to her headaches and back pain. Like so many patients, she was unaware of the power of her images and how negative they were.

We told Cyndi that sometimes symptoms are the body's way of communicating with us. Symptoms such as headaches and bad backs are tools that the body uses to bring a problem to our attention. Symptoms can be the body's way to alert us so that we can take action to prevent further injury and damage. We told Cyndi that neither her headaches nor her backaches were the enemy. Rather, they were clear signals that something in her life needed to change. We cautioned her that if she didn't do something, her symptoms could worsen or multiply.

We taught both Sam and Cyndi the LifeSkill we call visualizing success. It's practiced exactly as it sounds. We asked each of them to discard their negative images of failure and instead picture themselves being successful. We asked Sam to imagine that he made a successful decision. We had him picture himself as confident and capable as he went into his boss's office and announced his decision. We had him visualize a positive relationship with his daughter as they began a new life together. Cyndi's assignment was similar. We asked her to imagine that she navigated her morning and evening routines with aplomb. We then had her imagine driving to work and congratulating herself for managing her morning so well. For both of these patients, visualizing success was enormously helpful.

This LifeSkill works in two distinct and powerful ways. First, visualizing success relaxes and calms the body. Sam and Cyndi were reminded that visualizing success should be contrasted with their habitual visualizing of failure and pain. Their well-practiced failure-images led to stress, while images of success would lead to calmness and peace. Both people found their new images of success to be balms for their tired and stressed bodies.

Many studies back up our contention that positive imagery helps reduce pain and relaxes the body. In a study with a group of patients suffering from tension headaches, the imagery group was three times as likely to report major pain reduction. In other studies, positive visualization significantly reduced pain in patients with cancer, arthritis, fibromyalgia, hemophilia, and migraine headaches. In all these studies, the improvements in pain, physical function, and mental outlook were sustained for as long as eighteen months.

Positive imaging also helps in another powerful way. Visualizing success allows us to create better solutions for our problems. It helps us plan and anticipate creative outcomes to problems that have frustrated our best efforts. We all know people who use positive imagery; they seem to accomplish things by the force of their will. A well-known Italian psychiatrist, Dr. Rudolph Assagioli, found that successful people use specific steps that include clarification, deliberation, choice, affirmation, planning, and acting on the plan. Assagioli found that people who have trouble acting effectively tend to have a weakness in one or another of these steps. Some people struggle because they aren't clear on what they want to do; others, because they can't think of enough options; and still others, because they have difficulty choosing a path of action.

Sam and Cyndi are both examples of people who could neither clarify their intentions nor make wise choices. They didn't plan well, nor did they affirm their goals. They were both inept in each of the phases necessary for creating success. To demonstrate how the LifeSkill of visualizing success is used, let's focus for a minute on how we helped Cyndi.

Our first step was to make sure Cyndi was clear about her goal. She needed to be able to say exactly what it was she wanted to improve. After thinking for a bit, she was very clear that she wanted to be able to spend quality time with her kids without being stressed for time.

After she made her goal clear, we asked her to brainstorm ideas that might move her in the direction of success. Doing this gave her options whereby she could at least contemplate getting out of her rut. We asked her to try an experiment with us. That experiment was to picture herself as a successful parent. We asked her to picture a Cyndi who was capable of getting her life in order. We asked her to picture herself getting through her routines more efficiently and asked her to think of specific ways she might be more successful. After a brief practice of this, we went for the home run and asked Cyndi to picture a truly perfect day.

We asked her to describe to us exactly what she saw. We wanted to know what that kind of day looked like, in her eyes. We wanted to know precisely what she would have to do to create such a day. We wanted her to know those things too—wanted her to learn from the intelligence in her own mind. We wanted her to see that when she was calm, she could imagine her life working. And we wanted to affirm her ability to use her mind to creatively solve the problems in her life. When she became clear about how she could accomplish her day without it being a losing battle, we asked her to affirm the possibility of living her visualized success.

Cyndi then made a plan for how she could carry out the positive image, how she could change it from fantasy to reality. We asked her to consider what specific steps were involved and to lay out the order in which those steps would need to be taken. Finally, when she had a reasonable plan of action, we asked her to rehearse her plan again in her imagination. We wanted her to see success, to understand what it took to be successful, and to be able to go into her own imagination for answers.

This whole process took less than ten minutes. In that time Cyndi went from feeling helpless to having options. She went from feeling overwhelmed to experiencing hope. Her body relaxed, and for the first time we saw a smile on her face. She not only saw that it was possible to succeed; she felt hopeful in her calm body. Cyndi found wisdom in her own mind that was unavailable to her when she pictured herself as a failure. Visualizing success made available to Cyndi ideas she had never thought of before. When she could see herself as successful, she was able to figure out what it would take to create that experience. Then she rehearsed the successful experience in her mind as she moved through her day—even in the midst of noisy kids and tight time pressures. With some practice of her new LifeSkill, she found that her headaches went away and she was able to get her kids off to school on time.

Moving Cyndi from insight to action was the critical step in her success. During the moments of visualizing successful steps and outcomes, she was able to stay calm and relaxed. As she visualized a new way to deal with her children, she clarified her insights, brainstormed new options, and chose to go in a positive direction. Through the practice of visualizing success, she calmly rehearsed successful strategies until they were perfected.

Our ability to visualize better solutions to stressful problems is the missing link between those problems and successful solutions. Both Cyndi and Sam visualized success, thereby reclaiming their futures. They connected an old problem to a new solution and made positive changes in their lives. More important, both regained loving family relationships they had lost due to stress and their sense of failure. Those relationships were and are the true measure of their success.

LifeSkill Exercise:
Visualize Success

Purpose

The purpose of this LifeSkill is . . .

- To find better ways to achieve your goals.
- To feel successful about the things you do.
- To create better choices and options.

Practice

1. Think of some part of your life at which you're not successful.
2. Take three slow, full belly-breaths.
3. Picture in your mind succeeding at your chosen activity.
4. Describe to yourself what the successful picture showed you about how to succeed.
5. Think about how success was different from the things you usually do.
6. Now plan how you can put into practice what you saw.

Tips

- Start small and then gradually move on to bigger challenges.

- Practice this exercise at least three times for any one problem—more, if what you're working on is important.
- Write down the ideas of success that come to you.
- Take the time to really "see" the specific positive outcome you desire.

Application

Use this LifeSkill . . .

- Before going into an important meeting.
- When asking your boss for a raise or promotion.
- Before an important conversation with a friend, family member, or colleague.
- When working to develop a better golf swing or tennis return.
- When dieting or changing exercise patterns.
- When in a conflict that you'd like to see end with a win-win outcome.

"VISUALIZE SUCCESS" LIFESKILL:

Research shows us that when we picture ourselves being successful, we're more likely to accomplish our goals and dreams.

CHAPTER 7

Slow Down

Almost everyone we work with says they don't have enough time. They feel too busy, they say there are too many demands on their time, or they complain that work takes all their energy. This description fits Sally, who was a mother to three young children, as well as Milt, whose children had already gone off to college. Mark, a college student, felt short of time, as did Louise, who was retired. Almost everyone we've worked with or know feels overwhelmed. People everywhere complain of having too much to do and not enough time to do it. Being in a hurry is a normal state for most of us. The problem is that this constant hurrying creates more stress than it eliminates, and it doesn't even necessarily mean we get more done.

Sally couldn't imagine sitting down to enjoy a quiet lunch. Her children wanted her attention every moment, and she felt guilty on those few occasions that she didn't give it to them. Milt, on the other hand, couldn't imagine eating dinner without reading the business reports he didn't get to during the day. Louise thought that if she wasn't busy all the time, she was wasting her retirement, and Mark took extra classes and worked two jobs to get ahead. Each of these busy people accomplished a lot, yet each wondered why he or she wasn't getting enough enjoyment out of life.

The answer is simple: none of them has learned the importance of the LifeSkill we call slowing down. There's a wonderful line from a Simon and Garfunkel song that distills this process: "Slow down, you move too fast; you've got to make the morning last." Learning to do things more slowly is simple, really, yet in our hectic lives this approach is often neglected. Louise said she was successful in her life because she could do three things at once, and Milt was convinced that his career flourished because he accomplished as much as he could in as little time as possible. Sally felt too busy to even contemplate doing things more slowly.

The LifeSkill of slowing down reminds us of what we miss when we're in a hurry. For example, Sally usually felt so overwhelmed that she missed many of the delights of parenthood. Milt made a lot of money but rarely relaxed, and Louise, even though retired, never felt like she had enough time. Mark was so focused on doing well in school that he couldn't understand the concept of enjoying what he was doing at the time he was doing it. Each person was successful in some ways and a failure in others. When we saw them, the successes felt hollow and the strain was apparent.

The dilemma each of us faces is how to accomplish all that we have on our plates without losing our peace and joy. In our busy lives, that's no easy task. The bottom line is this:

even if we have more to do than time to do it in, we don't benefit when we rush around like chickens with our heads cut off. It's important to work productively, of course, since we all have many tasks we need to accomplish. However, it's only by slowing down that we get a glimpse of life's deepest gifts.

In some ways, affirming our perpetual need to hurry to get things done is like saying an operation was a success but the patient died. We all die a little when we finish a report on time but raise our blood pressure in doing so.

Dr. John Laragh of Cornell Medical School is one of the world's foremost blood pressure researchers. He was featured on the cover of *Time* magazine in 1975 for his discovery that renin, an enzyme released by the body when we're under stress, leads to increased blood pressure. Based on Dr. Laragh's work, a new group of drugs was developed that blocks renin and thereby controls blood pressure. Despite that background, Dr. Laragh has been a major proponent of using non-drug therapies such as relaxation methods to help reduce blood pressure. One such method is the LifeSkill of slowing down, which has been shown to be a highly effective and efficient way to decrease blood pressure.

Slowing down is very simple; it's only the practice that requires effort. In this chapter, as with all of the others, we ask you to practice what we teach. Daily and sustained practice of the LifeSkills enables you to develop a level of emotional competence that will successfully guide you through life's ups and downs.

One of the negative effects of hurrying is that you fail to make time for your family, children, and friends. You also miss the beauty of sunsets, fall colors, and the pattern of rain on the window. The good news is that the benefits of slowing down are instantaneous, and they accrue even with small changes. Slowing down can begin with something as simple as paying attention to what you eat. Instead of wolfing down a breakfast burrito in the car, or rushing into the local takeout joint to eat amid the hubbub, you can easily take a minute to taste and savor what you consume.

Rushing and not paying attention to the food we eat can lead to serious problems. It's one thing to fail to savor the full aroma and flavor of a single taco but another to gulp down Big Macs every day for lunch because we're always in a hurry. Research suggests that eating too fast is a factor contributing to the rising obesity epidemic in the United States. When we eat too fast, the brain doesn't have sufficient time to tell the stomach that it's full. Without that warning, we eat way beyond true hunger, and weight gain is the result.

Another problem with eating too fast is that it's often a poor attempt to manage stress. We all know the full, sleepy, relaxed feeling that we get after eating large holiday dinners. Many people overeat routinely as a way to try to capture that feeling (and therefore feel less stress). Unfortunately, overeating, and all of the extra calories that come with it, is an ineffective way to slow down and soothe our distress. In fact, overeating *causes* more stress than it *manages*. Having another helping of french fries because we feel rushed is dangerous to our health. Granted, when we're tired or in a hurry, it's difficult to remember the subtleties of the food pyramid. Making good food choices takes time and energy. But since good food choices, and the time to savor them, are necessary for our good health, it's time and energy well spent.

While gulping down a Whopper once in a while is fine, making consistently poor food choices and routinely eating too much has terrible consequences. Obesity is an enormous and growing health problem in the United States for both adults and children. Sally, whom we met earlier in this chapter, knew she should feed her children and herself better, but when she was running late, pizza and hamburgers were all she could manage. She hated the fact that she had gained fifteen pounds since Nick, her first child, was born. Mack, her husband, ate whatever was placed in front of him, and he too had put on weight. They both attributed their weight gain to being too busy to eat right. When we saw Sally at the clinic, we told her we thought this was too high a price to pay.

For each of you reading this book, there's an easy way to determine if you're too rushed and unfocused to enjoy your day. Please ask yourself these few simple questions:

- Have I recently had a conversation with someone and, moments later, forgotten what we talked about?

- Have I recently eaten my food so fast I had a queasy stomach afterward?
- Can I remember what I had for lunch yesterday?
- At the end of the day, do I wonder what I accomplished in the preceding hours?
- Do I often find myself saying, "I simply don't have enough time"?
- Do I feel that I often am missing something even when doing things I enjoy?
- When I'm talking to people, do I often think not about their words but about things I have to do?

If even a couple of these questions elicit a yes response, you may be going too fast for your own good. If this is an unusual week and you're busier than normal, that's not a problem. However, if rushing through things is normal for you, your health and happiness will suffer unless you change your ways. You need to learn to slow down, and you need to practice this LifeSkill faithfully.

If you answered yes to several or most of the above questions, you may already be feeling the health consequences of your hurrying. A number of studies have consistently shown that people who are hurried and, in particular, interrupt conversations, have a much higher risk of both heart disease and heart attacks. This finding was first presented by Dr. Meyer Friedman and Dr. Ray Rosenman, two eminent cardiologists in San Francisco, in their pioneering book *Type A Behavior and Your Heart.* These researchers identified being rushed as the main problem. Later research has refined that idea and found that both time pressure and hostility are dangerous.

One recent study from Duke University found that people who are rushed and routinely interrupt conversations are up to seven times more likely to develop heart disease. These researchers found that such people are competitive, controlling, rushed, and hostile—all risks factors for heart disease. To change this negative pattern, the researchers created another study that incorporated the LifeSkill of slowing down. Participants were instructed to slow down and listen rather than rushing and interrupting to get on to the next topic or to control the conversation. That simple change had a powerful effect: results of this LifeSkill research showed that participants' blood pressure was lowered and their level of stress chemicals, such as renin, was reduced simply by slowing down and listening.

Now, if you're still unconvinced that slowing down will be helpful to you, here's a simple exercise by which you can test our claim. If a picture is worth a thousand words, this exercise will convince almost everyone there's much to be gained by slowing down. Start this experiment by putting in front of you about a half dozen raisins or something else that's small (not messy) and tasty. Then imagine that you're in a hurry and have only a few moments to grab something to eat before you need to run out the door. Go ahead and grab a couple of the raisins and quickly eat them. Ask yourself: How did those raisins taste?

Before you take another raisin, do the following:

- First, imagine that you have time to sit and eat at your leisure.
- Now pick up a raisin and take a moment to smell it.
- Next, notice the way your raisin looks; take in its color and texture.
- Then roll it around in your hand and see how it feels in your fingers and on your palm.
- Put it in your mouth and suck on it for a few seconds.
- Then bite down once, slowly and carefully, without chewing.
- Finally, eat the raisin slowly, paying attention to the flavors in your mouth.

Then ask yourself: How did *that* raisin taste?

Almost everyone has a better experience eating the second raisin than the first raisins. Some people say they're amazed by how much sensation and pleasure they got out of eating one raisin. Other people remark that they've never fully *tasted* a raisin before. We assume that when you tried the experiment yourself, you noticed that raisins taste better, and you feel better, when you slow down. This simple lesson can be applied to both the small and the great activities of your life. The take-away message is this: our routine tasks provide rich experiences when we take the time to enjoy them.

Slowing down means doing whatever you're doing with

attention and care. Slowing down means doing one thing at a time. Slowing down means paying attention to what you're doing and thinking as little as possible about whatever else you have to do. Slowing down means doing *everything*, no matter what it is, as if that task is important. We showed Sally that even her laundry could be done with calm attention. When she tried it, she noticed how much that lessened her stress. She realized that when she was not thinking of the twelve other chores awaiting her, she could experience a sense of calm while completing even such a mundane task, and she could complete it efficiently.

Slowing down can be practiced anytime and anywhere. It's one of the most powerful tools we've found for reducing stress and increasing happiness. We asked Louise to begin by paying attention to what she ate and then to slow down as she washed dishes. Our suggestion to Mark was to leave his Walkman behind next time he went running and pay attention to his breathing instead. We asked Milt to stop for a moment after reading each business memo and reflect upon what was in the memo. Sally was asked to watch how her children explored their world and to see if she could observe them without becoming impatient.

Please understand that it's not necessary to slow down all day long. What is necessary is to have an OFF switch that allows you to slow down when you choose to. There are innumerable benefits to being able to slow down and pay attention. The stress you feel from not having enough time comes not only from your hurrying but also from your mind's constant message: "You have so much to do and not enough time." When you slow down, you put less strain on your body; therefore, you have more energy to accomplish your tasks. You also put less strain on your mind. Think back to the previous chapter on visualization. Remembering how negative messages affect your well-being, you can understand how dangerous it is to repeat over and over, "I don't have enough time."

If you want an easy reminder of the problem with negative self-talk, try this simple practice. Close your eyes and picture yourself late for a meeting (with meetings stacked up all day long). Forcefully remind yourself that you have too much to do and not enough time to do it. Your whole body will tense up and your heart will start to race. That's negativity in action.

Now shift gears. Take a deep breath and say something positive: "I have all the time I need." That affirmation is another way to practice slowing down. Notice how quickly your body and mind relax when you say something calming.

Slowing down is a wonderful practice. We've found that the most important area of life in which to apply this skill is relationships. Being positively involved with your family, children, spouse, friends, and colleagues is the single best stress buffer there is. Knowing that someone is concerned about you makes the hard times easier to bear and the good times better. People who are involved with other people are not only happier, they tend to be healthier and live longer. Unfortunately, too many people let their hurrying and busyness keep them from creating enduring relationships. Keeping up with the demands of life stops many of us from giving enough time to friends and family. Others, burned by problems with friends and relatives in the past, don't feel they have the energy to try again.

We're here to remind you that people are worth the effort. We *all* need people, whether we're young or old, single or married, at the top of the heap or just starting out. Fortunately, making and keeping close friends is a talent you can improve with practice. The LifeSkill of slowing down and paying attention will help you get closer to people.

Milt came to us complaining that he didn't have enough support in his life. He felt unappreciated and believed that people took him for granted. His relationship with his wife felt stale and predictable, and he didn't have time for his friends.

As a starting point, we asked Milt what he thought accounted for his lack of support. We asked him to reflect on the two most common reasons we've encountered:

1. You know how to make friends but simply don't have enough time.
2. You've tried to make friends or get closer to the friends and relatives you have, but you end up feeling hurt.

Milt responded immediately that these were in fact the reasons he felt unappreciated and alienated. We suggested to him that he find time to slow down and pay attention to the social experiences he had every day.

We asked Milt to have a five-minute conversation with his wife every day—a *real* conversation focused exclusively on her. That meant no eating, watching TV, reading, or being otherwise distracted while talking and listening. We also suggested that he ask her if she felt he was paying enough attention to the conversation. At first, Milt said he found these instructions both difficult and annoying. He resented giving his wife "power," as he put it, and was uncomfortable with a conversation unaccompanied by other activity. He persevered, however, and eventually found both the conversation and the quiet rewarding.

In addition to using his new LifeSkill in conversation with his wife, we suggested that he apply it with his other family members and associates, including his business partners and his college-age daughters. We suggested that he pay attention—that is, listen without multitasking—whenever one of his daughters was on the telephone. We also suggested that he set aside time at least once each week to meet a friend for lunch or dinner and focus part of the conversation on anything but business. In addition, we suggested that he spend some part of his business meetings asking associates how their lives were going. We told Milt that as long as he was in relationships, more of him should show up than his clothing and his day-planner.

Milt found learning to slow down and pay attention helpful in addressing both aspects of his social alienation. As he slowed down when relating, he started to give people more attention. The upshot was he noticed that people had more attention to offer him. He got more out of his conversations, and people were more interested in conversing with him. Milt also learned that the simple act of slowing down and paying attention meant he was a better listener when his wife and daughters talked.

Slowing down and listening turned out to be a powerful tool for improving Milt's business relationships, and it also reduced his many resentments. He no longer felt isolated and misunderstood. He learned to let people know he understood their point of view and had heard their feelings. He found that it was more rewarding to pay attention to the person he was talking to than to keep five things going all the time in his mind.

Like Milt, you can learn how to slow down and pay attention. The results for you, as for him, will include reduced stress, better relationships, and lower blood pressure.

LifeSkill Exercise: Slow Down

Purpose

The purpose of this LifeSkill is . . .

- To put less strain on your body.
- To free up more energy to accomplish what you need to do.
- To allow time to appreciate all that your life has to offer.

Practice

1. Do a common activity slowly, carefully, and with focused attention. Start by taking a couple of slow, deep belly-breaths. Then pay close attention to how good something smells (a rose or some food); notice how beautiful something looks (nature, a loved one, or a piece of art); look carefully at every aspect of something (the marvel of your hands, for example). Drink in wonderful tastes, colors, shapes, and textures.
2. When you're in a hurry, tell yourself, "I have all the time that I need."

Tips

- Sometimes speed up what you're doing so that you can notice how uncomfortable that feels.
- Practice doing something the usual way and then slow down and practice again.
- Remind yourself that you can't go any faster than the maximum you're capable of.
- Notice slower breathing and greater calmness whenever you practice slowing down.
- Observe that food tastes better when eaten slowly.
- You'll find that family and friends will appreciate you more when you slow down to talk and listen to them.

Application

Use this LifeSkill . . .

- When waiting in line in a grocery store or airline security area.
- When rushing to an appointment.
- When you notice you are driving too fast.
- When drinking wine, so that you can really taste the flavor.
- When you feel impatient.
- When you feel bored.
- When making dinner for friends, family, or yourself.

"SLOW DOWN" LIFESKILL:

Slowing down and being absolutely focused on what you're doing is one of the most effective ways to manage stress and manifest both health and happiness.

CHAPTER 8

Appreciate Yourself

This chapter builds upon the skills introduced in Chapter 4, which focused on the power of counting your blessings. We want to reiterate that the purpose of our Stress Free program is not just to reduce your stress (and thus the wear and tear on your body), but also to help you become a happier person. That's why Stress Free is more than just a stress management training program.

We consider developing the many facets of the skill of appreciation to be a cornerstone of our Stress Free program and the cornerstone of a happier life. Chapter 4 instructed you to notice the beauty in your surroundings and the good things in your life. This simple practice is helpful for reducing stress and increasing happiness. This new LifeSkill focuses on appreciating *you*—the good you do, the love you offer, and the ways you make the world a better place.

Most of the people we see in the clinic come to us with physical complaints of one sort or another. We see people, like Sarah, suffering from high blood pressure due to poor eating habits, overwork, age, and difficult family circumstances.

Or Eric, whose stress-induced back pain is so severe that he gets through the day only by taking ibuprofen morning and night. Or Janet, who is trying to juggle school, kids, divorce, and a job that triggers exhaustion, a short temper, and headaches. Each person we see tells us his or her troubles and describes specific stresses. We listen, we offer concern for the pain each person is experiencing, and we suggest strategies for improvement. Often, though, we're struck by something else—something unspoken—that's the underlying problem or real issue for these people.

That "something else" is that most people just aren't happy enough. They're not getting enough joy out of their lives. This may sound like a given—people who come into a clinic to see psychologists aren't happy enough—but it's important enough that we see it as a distinct symptom.

Janet didn't come right out and talk about that missing "something else," but it was apparent when she spoke with us. Her sense of being overwhelmed was palpable, though she didn't use the word *happy* or *unhappy* while describing the frequency and duration of her headaches. She used words like *stressed, tired, overwhelmed,* and *obligated.* What we heard in addition to these words was a simple plea for greater happiness. Underneath her discussion of the headaches and stress was a desire to *enjoy* her life more.

We found the same experience with Ellen. Her primary complaint was angina pain. The chest pains she experienced when she exerted herself scared her to death. There was a real basis for her fears, since researchers know that stress can reduce the blood flow to the heart as much as can physical exertion. Since there was no medical evidence of Ellen's having heart disease, it was her excessive worry that was creating angina by limiting blood flow to her heart. Ellen was fearful of new experiences and even of going too far from home. She clung to her husband when faced with stress and generally restricted her life to deal with both her pain and her fear. But beneath the concerns that Ellen voiced about her heart and the pain of the angina, we heard a woman lamenting the lack of happiness in her life. Again, she didn't come out and say *unhappy*, but we heard it nonetheless. We hear this plea from *most* of our patients, and we address it directly with teachable skills such as self-appreciation.

Appreciating yourself is another LifeSkill whose aim is to help you to enjoy and relish your everyday life. This practice asks you to appreciate the many things you do each day that are loving and/or helpful. Many people struggle to appreciate themselves; they rarely acknowledge the good they do and the routine talents they demonstrate. This LifeSkill reminds us that we all do a number of things each day that are worthy of recognition. It's far too easy to take ourselves for granted. People don't have to invent a cure for cancer or have a fancy job or a big house to appreciate what they do and the talents they have. And if they learn to appreciate those things, they avoid one of the prime causes of the unhappiness.

We assert that for most of our patients, greater happiness is possible. Now, greater happiness doesn't mean that their lives will be easy all the time. In fact, wanting a life without difficulty is a surefire path to *un*happiness. We didn't envision a trouble-free future when we counseled Janet, for example. We didn't minimize the pressure she felt, the many things she had to accomplish, or the headaches she suffered (which were a legitimate cause for concern). Janet had a lot on her plate and didn't have a lot of support.

Likewise, we were fully aware of how frightening it was for Ellen to have chest pain. Being sick is scary and painful. We knew that Eric's job was a bear and that his boss was intimidating. We also knew that with two small children he couldn't quit his current job, no matter how much he wanted to. With these examples and others, such as the loss of a job or the death of a family member, suffering is appropriate. The question is always how much suffering and for how long.

Some people whose unhappiness is ongoing suffer from severe or morbid depression. These folks require medical and/or psychological treatment to feel better. (For severe depression, it's clear from current research that a combination of psychotherapy and appropriate medications works better than either approach alone.) Most of us, though, can find greater happiness, despite life's difficulties, simply by honing our appreciation skills.

When people become used to seeing the glass as half empty, they forget that it can be seen as half full and need to be reminded periodically. Another way of saying this is that happiness can be taught and then practiced—even in a life fraught with difficulty. Simple skills like appreciation lead people to have more positive experiences. The LifeSkill of self-appreciation produces immediate results in reducing stress and enhancing well-being, and with a little practice it leads to greater contentment.

Remember, feeling good doesn't have to be as difficult as we tend to make it. Life is stressful, no doubt about it, and managing that stress is a necessity of life. But it's *doable*. Remember how good it feels to actually overcome a difficulty or impediment in your life? As good as that feels, it's not enough. That's simply managing to break even, which is necessary but not sufficient; it's only *part* of the solution. Finding and living a life of greater happiness is the other part, and it must be practiced.

Sarah was a sixty-year-old schoolteacher who did extra duty caring for her husband, Jim. A retired firefighter, Jim had left his job four years earlier when his rheumatoid arthritis worsened. Jim wasn't crippled, but his mobility was reduced and he was in pain. Sarah and Jim had three grown children and five grandchildren. Their kids were devoted and brought the grandkids regularly to visit. Sarah had taught elementary school for twenty-five years, and her retirement was still a few years away. She needed to continue teaching for the benefits package and for the ongoing income. Her husband's pension wasn't large, and their medical expenses were high.

Sarah came to us because she had developed high blood pressure. Though this symptom becomes more common as people age, up until a year earlier Sarah's blood pressure had been normal. At a routine visit with her gynecologist the previous year, her blood pressure was found to be elevated, and it had been rising since. Since Jim's retirement, she had put on fifteen pounds and for the first time in her life couldn't lose the extra weight when she tried. One of the ways Sarah dealt with the cards she'd been given, she admitted, was to eat richer foods and bigger portions. As discussed earlier, people often try to sedate themselves with food in order to reduce their stress. While that too-full feeling does temporarily reduce stress, it increases the waistline.

Everyone who met Sarah thought she was a delightful woman—warm, nurturing, and kind. However, she described herself as tired and stressed out. All too often, she reported, she felt a sense of urgency and impatience, as though her life were passing her by. This was a warning sign to us, since a very large study of heart disease in 2003 (the CARDIA project) found that a sense of time urgency and impatience leads to increased blood pressure. Sarah talked of having outlived her usefulness as a teacher. She told us that almost all of the teachers her age had retired over the past few years. She struggled because she was the age of her principal's mother and the age of her co-teachers' grandmothers. She referred to the increase in her blood pressure as a sure indication of her mortality and of the inevitable diminishments of age. All in all, Sarah was a discouraged woman, and our job was to help her appreciate herself more.

Seeing the good in Sarah wasn't a difficult task. After listening to her pain, fear, and struggles, we reflected back to her that we saw a hero in front of us. We started to list all the things she was doing to help other people. We highlighted the incredible service she rendered to her husband—the patience she showed, the kindness, and the daily work of helping him adapt to his illness. We commented on her continuing to teach small children and the obvious care she had for them. We reminded her of her close family ties to children and grandchildren. We told her that in our eyes she was brave and inspiring. Her fortitude touched us and we actually called her a hero. She was hard working under adverse conditions and helped a good number of people. She simply was unable to see all the good she did and how important her life was. As our meeting progressed and she still couldn't appreciate herself, we asked her to answer two questions:

1. What would the world lose if you stopped doing all that you do?
2. Do you wish to see the cup of your life as half full or half empty?

These two questions are linked. The first asks us to look at who is helped by our daily actions. Sarah had many people for whom she made a difference—her husband, her children, her grandchildren, the children in her class, and their parents. The second question implies that each of us has some degree of choice about how we feel. And that's true: we can choose to practice appreciation; we can learn to pay attention to the ways in which we enrich the world. We can't always make things better, but we can *feel* better about them, and we can continue to work for good. As Sarah practiced the LifeSkill of self-appreciation, her blood pressure gradually returned to normal over the course of the next three months.

The key to making this exercise work—and work powerfully—is understanding that what we appreciate about ourselves doesn't have to be a big deal. Our goodness doesn't have to be the stuff of movies or TV shows. If you want to model your goodness after a movie, pass up *Superman* and use *It's a Wonderful Life*. In that classic movie, the Jimmy Stewart character, George, found that the good deeds of his life were remembered by the people he'd helped and that he'd profoundly influenced their lives. We don't have to write the Great American Novel or have an exciting job to be useful and important. We just have to do things that help someone or some cause or ourselves. And the good news is that we all do. We all contribute more than we might imagine to our family, our friends, our community, and ourselves. The things that make a difference are so simple it's no wonder most of us pass them by.

Our goodness rests in doing the laundry and cooking dinher and going to the grocery store and cleaning up after the children. It's found in getting gas for the car and offering patience to our family members. It's waking up on Saturday to play with our kids and staying up late to talk with friends or lovers. It's going to work to support our family or calling a friend to ask how he or she is feeling. It's reminding ourselves at work that what we do helps someone who receives our services. It's doing our work with a remembrance of our desire to help. It's volunteering at our child's school or sending a check to charity. It's making sure our partners and spouses feel appreciated. It's giving them a back rub when they're worn out. The good we do is everywhere; we just have to look for it. When we look for it, we will find it. When we find it, we will discover own small piece of heroism, without which the world wouldn't be the same.

As you learn the LifeSkill of appreciating yourself, we remind you to pay attention to your self-talk. You can choose what you tell yourself about your life. Do you tell yourself that you're a failure? That you haven't accomplished enough? Do you put yourself down for mistakes and imperfections that are just part of being human? When something goes wrong, do you imagine that you've blown it big-time? If you do all these things, then it's no surprise that you feel stressed and unappreciated. On top of the stress of your life experiences, you're adding additional stress in what you're telling yourself. Remember: you always have a *choice* about what you tell yourself.

Craig, who came for a consultation at our clinic, was an overworked and underappreciated accountant with severe back pain. He told us about getting a note that said that his supervisor wanted to speak with him. A negative thinker, Craig immediately concluded that he must have done something wrong. He tried to remember every little project on which he might have made a mistake. Talking to himself in this way made him feel nervous about meeting with his supervisor, put a knot in his stomach, and made it hard for him to concentrate on his work.

This is a classic example of the Type 2 stress response brought on by a person's imagination. In reality, the note Craig received asking him to see the supervisor didn't make him upset; his own thinking did! He imagined the worst-case scenario rather than expecting the best or at least approaching the meeting with a neutral, wait-and-see attitude.

How different would Craig's life have been if he'd thought more about the good that he did? If he'd realized that the work he did had great importance to his children and his wife? That his clients benefited from his expertise and he got a daily opportunity to solve problems. What Craig *thought* directly affected how he *felt*. Unfortunately, Craig tended to focus on the negative possibilities and aspects of a situation, ignoring the positive. Craig told himself it was best to prepare for the worst possibility; by focusing on that, he could avoid disappointment. However, this kind of thinking had become so habitual that he thought negative thoughts even about situations that weren't bad at all. Because of this, he regularly missed opportunity after opportunity to appreciate what he did and how he did it.

This last aspect of self-appreciation highlights the things we do well. It's easy to remember the things we fail at and/or the habits that cause us difficulty. We're forced to pay attention if we have the habit of neglecting to pay our bills and get letters from collection agencies. We're forced to pay attention if we eat too much candy and the dentist tells us we have cavities. But it's equally (if not more) important to be honest about our skills and strengths. This doesn't mean you should get a swelled head and walk around telling everyone you're an excellent cook or a dynamite accountant or whatever. It just means regularly appreciating, in the quiet of your heart and mind, your own special skills; it means realizing that each one of us is talented in our own unique way.

As with the good we do, our skills don't have to be a big deal. Craig, for example, was an excellent Little League coach but not much of an athlete. If he reminded himself how poor his coordination was, he felt unhappy. If he reminded himself how well he worked with children, he felt satisfaction. We asked him to reflect regularly on how good he was with children. We knew this would make him happier and reduce his stress.

Sarah was a phenomenal grandmother. What does it take to be a good grandmother? To Sarah the qualifications included having patience and offering her time. She could watch the same video four times in a row with her five-year-old grandson without getting bored. She could sit on the floor with her three-year-old granddaughter and play with toys hour after hour.

Are these skills by themselves a big deal? No. Are they worthy of admiration? Yes. And we made sure that Sarah knew we thought so. We asked her to list playing with grandchildren with patience and care among her many skills. Then we suggested that she be proud of these accomplishments. Yes, she was older than most of the people she worked with—but most of them would find watching a video over and over boring and most of them would find watching a three-year-old sort colors uninteresting. Not Sarah. These skills were her unique gift at this time in her life. The more she understood this concept, the happier she was and the less stressed she felt.

It's one thing to do the laundry, and it's another thing to do the laundry well. It's one thing to cook, and it's another thing entirely to cook with care and passion. It's one thing to read books, and it's another thing to have read all the writings of a particular author and be able to make inferences about his work. It's one thing to own a home, and it's another thing to make it beautiful. We all do some things well. It's necessary to our health and happiness that we recognize those skills.

Finally, sometimes it's enough simply to try hard. Sometimes our skill is perseverance. Sometime the simple act of not giving up is both a skill and a virtue. We can be good at trying, and if we are, we need to honor our effort. Darlene wasn't a great baker, but did her kids care that the brownies weren't perfect? George wasn't a world-class carpenter, but did his son care about that when George was always ready to lend a helping hand? Even when George didn't know how to fix something, to his son he was still a hero.

The point of self-appreciation is to get into the habit of finding positive things to think about yourself. Positive things you do are there for the finding. Remember the good you do and acknowledge yourself. Remember the good you do and take a break from stress. Remember the good you do and feel happier. You deserve it!

LifeSkill Exercise:
Appreciate Yourself

Purpose

The purpose of this LifeSkill is . . .

- To notice the many good things you do.
- To learn to appreciate your talents and skills.
- To remind yourself that you work hard and are worthy of praise.

Practice

Reflect back on your day:

1. Think of one or two things you did that were helpful or that you were good at.
2. Appreciate yourself for your talents and willingness to help.
3. Realize that offering kindness, help, and support are all positive choices that you make.
4. Even little things need to get done. Appreciate yourself for not having blown them off.

Tips

- It's easy to forget how much good we do, such as visiting someone who is sick, listening to a friend, doing the laundry, or making dinner.

- We're often criticized for things we do wrong rather than praised for things we do right. Look for your own virtues if all you're hearing is complaints.
- It can be difficult for others to acknowledge that someone is doing things well or being kind. Sometimes you have to do it for yourself.
- Remember that appreciation isn't the same as conceit.

Application

Use this LifeSkill . . .

- When you feel inferior at a social or business meeting.
- At the end of the day, if you're wondering what you accomplished.
- When you feel that your abilities aren't being appreciated at work.
- When you feel overlooked by others.
- When doing a hobby.
- When caring for your children.

"APPRECIATE YOURSELF" LIFESKILL:

Learning to appreciate your own worth and value isn't an indulgence; it's seeing clearly your own unique character and gifts.

CHAPTER 9

Smile Because You Care

Most of the patients we see are good at telling us what's wrong in their lives. Generally speaking, that's why they come to see us, after all. Understandably, people rarely go to clinics to tell physicians and psychotherapists how *well* their lives are going, how *good* they feel, or how *little* strain they're under. No, we see few people living stress-free lives. Most of our patients regale us with stories about the pressure they're under, which they suggest is caused by the chores, work, people, and responsibilities that make up their daily lives.

To us and our patients, both pieces of information are useful. It's important that they know what's wrong in their lives (and are able to articulate it), but it's equally important that they honor the responsibilities and meet the demands they face. The problem is that almost all of our patients miss the power that comes from recognizing how much of what they do is done because they love their family, friends, and community, or because they have a desire to make the world a better place. As we've mentioned in previous chapters, they miss the myriad demonstrations of the power of appreciation for creating health and happiness.

The specific components of appreciation these patients miss are the love and care that underlie and motivate their daily work and business. One of our patients, Judy, had as her personal motto: "Thank God it's Monday." She felt so overwhelmed by her home responsibilities that she looked forward to Monday mornings, a time most people dread. At 8:00 A.M. on Monday, she could leave her home and enter her office, where there were people who assisted her—co-workers (frequently men) who brought her coffee, scheduled her appointments, and made sure that she had a good lunch. At work she felt collaborated with and sustained, while at home she ran on empty as she cared for everyone in her family. The LifeSkill of smiling because you care benefited Judy enormously.

Judy wasn't conscious of the fact that the work she did at home for her family grew out of her love for her husband and children. These strong feelings of love and care, if brought to the surface and remembered, can provide the necessary energy to work hard, be creative, endure difficulty, and persevere. Love and care do that for each of us. Taking care of people we love takes energy, but when we can recognize and acknowledge the love that is our true motivation, it connects us with our deepest purpose and soothes our stress. This LifeSkill worked for Judy, and it can work for you. The power of underlying love makes hard work meaningful and opens our hearts to the kindness inside us.

The fact that our patients miss the care and love that underlie their hard work is, we believe, a primary cause of their unhappiness and stress. Learning to recognize the good that each of us does *because we care* is the heart and soul of this LifeSkill. Learning to see the care, love, and affection in our daily actions and the actions of others is a critical ingredient in manifesting our optimal performance. We shake our heads regularly as we reflect on how simple this LifeSkill is and how profound its benefit. When we listen to people like Sally, who worked so hard to keep her family together, we wonder, "Why wasn't she taught the simple skill of tuning in to her own goodness and care to buffer her from life's inevitable stress?"

In Chapter 8 we reminded you to appreciate yourself. We asked you to notice the skills you have and to recognize the good that you do. We suggested that each of you is a hero in your life and that many people benefit from your actions. *This* LifeSkill builds on what we taught you in Chapter 8 by focusing on understanding that underneath the busyness and stress of your life there's a bounty of loving intentions that go uncultivated and unnoticed.

Take Sarah, whom we introduced in the previous chapter. She loved her husband enough to work full-time at a job for which she felt too old. She endured being a generation or two older than her peers. She loved her husband enough to attend to his needs and wants as his health deteriorated. Did Sarah recognize the depth of the emotions of love and care that lay behind her daily commitments? She did not. What she con-nected to was the stress of it all—and because of that, she suf-fered more than she had to. While the stress was certainly there, so too was a tremendous amount of love and care.

We find examples of care and kindness in almost every person we talk to. And yet we also find a corresponding fail-ure to appreciate the motivation behind the acts, which results in a sense of strain and lack of purpose. In so many cases that come to our attention, we see evidence that people suffer stress and burnout because they lose sight of their own goodwill. In a physical and metaphorical sense, they fail to take their own love to heart. They fail to benefit from the relaxation that occurs when they remember their love, and they pass up positive health benefits and a boost in self-esteem as well.

For example, Jodi was a full-time nurse and a mother to her two children, and she also helped care for her aged mother. When she saw us, it was because her blood pressure was elevated and she was worn out. Why was Jodi doing so much? Why was her plate so full? In part, it was because she was a responsible person and there was a lot to do. Someone needed to pay the bills and drive her mother to the doctor. Someone needed to make sure the kids' lunches were made and the food shopping got done. But this analysis misses the heart of the matter: at the core of Jodi's story is how she extended herself because she was committed to the well-being of her nuclear and extended family. When she recognized that tremendous love was the foundation of her hard work, her cardiovascular and nervous systems breathed sighs of relief.

Janet was a single parent who struggled to balance the relentless demands on her time. She got her kids up early and put them to bed late. In between she worked full-time, ran the family errands, cooked the family meals, did the family laundry, negotiated with her ex-husband, and tried to stay awake. She rarely, if ever, took the time to experience the power of the love she showed her children. Nor did she contemplate how intense that love must be as it manifested itself in the relentless energy she put out on their behalf. Janet thought she worked so hard because she *had* to. We knew better: we knew she worked hard and cared so much because of her deep and abiding love.

Edith was an attorney who worked long hours. She traveled a lot and lived a hectic and busy life. The company she worked for was involved in litigation that could help a good many people get money from a corrupt corporation. Her work required enormous intelligence and intensity, and Edith had both traits in abundance. She believed in what she was doing, and her passion showed. Unfortunately, so did her exhaustion and pain. Edith wasn't connected to the part of herself that cared enough to work hard to make the world a better place. She was lost in the details, the energy required, and her exhaustion.

Each of these women was intelligent, hard-working, determined, and exhausted. And each woman was experiencing

Type 2, prolonged stress in response to her hard work and dedication. Although the stress response is effective in the short run, as we saw earlier, it's exhausting if it goes on for too long. The women described above felt they were on a treadmill, dancing as fast as they could, with no end in sight. They missed what was at the heart of their life: a tremendous amount of care and love. They missed the central reality of their own experience. When they were able to slow down enough to recognize their already loving hearts, they found deserved peace and well-being.

Here's the way we showed Sarah how to practice smiling because she cared. We asked her to sit up straight and try to *feel* the love she had for her husband. We asked her to think about how much she did for him routinely—things such as cooking, shopping, going to work, listening as he talked about his discomfort, running errands, and so on. We asked her to realize that under all those obligations lay a tremendous force: the force of love, the force of caring. We asked her to recognize how great a role this profound love played in getting her out of bed every morning. Then, as she was thinking of this love, we asked her to bring a smile to her face. We told her that a smile deepens the power of this practice and works magic on its own. Once she had her instructions, the whole exercise took about fifteen seconds, and well within that time Sarah breathed a gentle and appreciative sigh of relief.

We asked her to practice regularly during the day and see what effect this LifeSkill had on her stress. We suggested that she do this when she was angry at work, stressed out by a traffic jam, or stuck on the phone with a rude customer service representative. We suggested that she do this before she walked through her door in the evening. We challenged her to do it often and report to us the results. We reminded her of the old adage that the best things in life are free. A smiling face costs nothing, nor does a full heart—and both are among the best things you can do for your health.

We learned about the healing power of a smile from a patient of ours. She had read about a Russian researcher who investigated a monastery that was having remarkable results with patients plagued by all forms of degenerative disease. Part of the therapy used at the monastery was smile therapy. Each individual, visitor and permanent resident alike, was required to have good posture and wear a smile at all times. That's right, they were *required* to smile—and it was powerfully effective. We know now that adding a smile to appreciation creates happiness and well-being—positive states of mind that we tell people are literally (and we mean *literally!*) right under their noses.

A smile is the expression of contentment and joy. When you feel happy, you smile. No other part of the body registers such a visible change. Research by Dr. Paul Ekman at the University of California School of Medicine in San Francisco has found that smiling registers in the part of the brain called the hypothalamus, where endorphins are produced and many hormones are regulated. Endorphins are naturally occurring opiates that relieve pain and give a sense of pleasure, peace, well-being, and even euphoria. According to Dr. Ekman's findings, smiles stimulate their production.

Try a smile right now. Think of the love you offer, and smile. Hold that smile for about ten seconds. Every person that we've asked to do this has reported feeling better. In other words, not only do you smile when you feel happy, but you feel happy when you smile! Apparently you can't have one without the other. So if you want to experience a moment of happiness, smile. If you have a hard time smiling out of the blue, think of a close member of your family or another loved one, and remember the last time you saw him or her laughing. With this image, you will smile. This is joy traveling outward. Now, if you want your joy to go inward, configure your face into a smile. A moment of good feeling will follow.

Have you ever grimaced after watching someone bang her knee or elbow? Have you smiled back at a child when he smiled at you? It turns out that this is an "empathy" response that's part of the wiring of the human brain. This was revealed in a new study by Dr. Christian Keysers at the University of Parma in Italy. He and his fellow researchers used a magnetic resonance imaging (MRI) instrument to observe the brains of test subjects who were watching short movies of people expressing both positive and negative emotions. In each instance, positive and negative, the part of the test subjects' brain that experiences pleasure and pain (the anterior insula) would light up. That response showed that people were empathizing with the people in the movies—that is, sharing their feelings. If we're all connected and influenced by the facial expressions of people . . . what more compelling reason could there be to smile?

Please understand: we're not suggesting that you paste on the insincere grin of a beauty pageant contestant. On the contrary, we're suggesting a warm, sincere smile. If this is difficult for you, you need to practice. If you need a reason to practice, remember that your smile will give someone you love and care about a real boost. Everyone responds to a smile. Do you want to enjoy your friends more? Smile more. Do you want to have more friends? Smile more. Do you want to get along better with your wife, husband, children, and other family members? Sincere smiles based in love will do the trick.

On the cover of the June 30, 2003, issue of *Newsweek* magazine, a young married couple was shown propped up in bed. He was looking at his laptop computer, she was eating ice-cream, and they were both frowning. The headline read, "No Sex, Please, We're Married." Inside was a feature story about why many young married couples have poor sex lives. It offered as primary reasons work, children, and stress, as if these were new to human experience.

Here's a question for you to ponder: Is the couple frowning because they have a poor sex life, or do they have a poor sex life because they're frowning? If they had warm, loving smiles on their faces, the headline would make no sense. Smiles can't create love where it doesn't exist, of course, but they change your brain chemistry enough that you can remember the love that stress has obscured. A smile on your face also creates an experience of safety for a loved one, helping that person to likewise find misplaced good feelings.

Following up on that idea, here's one more way to remind your face to smile. Shut your eyes and imagine that you're as loving as you wish to be and as loved as you wish to be. Visualize and feel that wonderful state of giving and getting all the love you want for about ten seconds. Then open your eyes. Did you smile? Of course you did. You *have* to smile when you feel love and when you feel that you are loved.

Jodi, Sally, Edith, and all others who have learned to smile because they care came to understand how love undergirded their hard work. Ultimately, each was able to show her care through a smile. We taught them to acknowledge and feel the care and love they already had. We taught each of these women to smile as they remembered their feelings of love. As mentioned in prior chapters, the relaxation from any of our LifeSkills takes about ten seconds to take effect. Even though the results are quick, they're profound. In fact, with practice they're life-altering. Each of these women attested to the power of this simple practice and the positive emotions they regularly felt. Each of these women was changed for the better.

Before we end the discussion of this LifeSkill, there's one

more benefit to smiling because you care that we wish to highlight. Remembering what we care for connects us to our deepest sense of purpose. So many of us are lost because our lives lack meaning and purpose. Edith was lost in the details of her demanding job and couldn't keep track of why she was working so hard. She was so overwhelmed by the daily grind that she lost her purpose. Simply getting to bed at a decent hour became her goal.

Edith went to work each day to help people who couldn't defend themselves. She didn't go to work solely to write legal briefs, nor did Sarah go to work simply to grade homework. Their purpose was to do good and help others, and their actions reflected that goal. They were living a purpose that they had lost sight of. Only when they reconnected with their deep reservoir of love and care could they see that their ship of life was pointed in the right direction. Edith was unable to see the forest for the tress until she remembered care and concern was her driving force.

We want to leave you with one caveat. The fact that you're filled with love and care and that your purpose is noble does *not* mean that you should remain in difficult or abusive situations. Remembering love is no substitute for protecting yourself from harm or stopping people from being cruel. Nothing in this chapter says that love means you have to stay in a situation no matter how poorly you're treated. Sometimes you do have to seek professional help for your problems, and sometimes in abusive situations you have to summon the police. In less extreme situations, though, a regularly practiced loving smile will increase your happiness, improve your health, and put you on the path to a peaceful and healthy life.

LifeSkill Exercise:
Smile Because You Care

Purpose

The purpose of this LifeSkill is . . .

- To reflect on the positive reasons you do most of the things in your life.
- To remind yourself that you care about people and show it.
- To realize the value of even your mundane tasks.
- To remember the loving reason behind all the good that you do.

Practice

Reflect back on your day:

1. Take a couple of slow, deep breaths.
2. Think of some tasks or chores that you did today.
3. Ask yourself why you did these things.
4. When you remember that you did them because you care, smile.
5. Think about how much you care about the people you do things for—and smile.
6. Feel your experience of love and care and let it warm the area around your heart—and smile again.

Tips

- Remember that often we do things because we want to be of help.
- Reflect on how much you care for all the people around you.
- Remember how much help you are to them.
- Think about how what you do would be missed if you stopped.
- Smile whenever you can for a mood lift.
- Smile at people, and they'll more likely smile at you.

Application

Use this LifeSkill . . .

- When you're feeling discouraged.
- When you're feeling overworked.
- When you're doing routine things like laundry or cooking or mowing the lawn.
- When you're down in the dumps.
- When you're being photographed.

"SMILE BECAUSE YOU CARE" LIFESKILL:

When you smile, your body and mind move into a healing state of peace and well-being—so care, and then smile.

CHAPTER 10

Stop Doing What Doesn't Work

Jack was a typical patient of ours. At forty-six years old, he made his first visit to the Stanford Preventive Cardiology clinic. Gregarious and warm, Jack wasn't sure why he had been sent to see medical psychologists. We discussed the mind/body connection with him and explained that we hoped to help him improve his overall health by reducing his stress level.

Jack had been working to control diabetes for ten years and recently had been told that he had an atrial arrhythmia as well. His doctor had often mentioned that the diabetes might be exacerbated by stress, and now he was wondering if the arrhythmia might also be related to stress. Jack had been complaining about the high level of stress in his life for years: he had an extremely demanding job and a problematic marriage. He clearly loved his wife and they cooperated well in their busy life. However, they both were so worn out and stressed that their relationship had suffered, and over time they had become less kind to each other.

In the ten years since Jack was diagnosed with diabetes, he had never found the time to take a stress management class, despite his doctor's repeated recommendation. He hadn't bothered to develop better eating or exercise habits either, which made controlling the diabetes difficult. Jack saw taking care of himself as something that fell in line behind work, chores, responsibilities, family, and friends.

Jack owned a farm in the Central Valley of California and worked painfully long hours. He found his work challenging, difficult, and consuming. He had no complaints about the actual work he did—he was good at managing the farm and liked the hands-on labor—but he resented the stress that came with it.

Jack had three children and a wife of seventeen years. Together with a few employees, they did all the work on their farm. Jack's stress arose from the long workdays, the vulnerability of his crops to weather, the ebbing demand for what he grew, the difficulty of retaining good employees, and the need to harvest crops at a specific, brief time of the year (sometimes under difficult conditions). His health also caused him stress. He was frustrated by the side effects of certain medications he took and by the doctor's exhortations to do something about his health without telling him exactly how to make those changes.

Jack told us that his work problems were an inherent part of the job of farming. Weather always had to be reckoned with, employees left and had to be replaced, crops were more or less in demand, and long hours were a given. This meant that the stressors in Jack's life were constant; they weren't going to change. Jack had no control over the weather, the demand for crops, or the changing lives of his employees. These long-term, unrelenting sources of stress were classic triggers of the destructive Type 2 stress response. In fact, many of the stressors were the same ones that had been faced by his father and grandfather before him, when *they* ran the farm. The problem, then, wasn't the immutable stressors; it was the fact that Jack did little or nothing to manage his stress.

We understood that there was little Jack could do to alter the nature of his business, but we wondered why he didn't change some of the ways he dealt with his farm. He couldn't determine the amount of rain per season, but he *could* change his habits and behaviors to better handle his intense level of stress. We knew we could help Jack if we could get him to talk more about his choices and less about his workplace demands. Our basic question to Jack was, "Okay, we hear that it's hard. Now, what are you doing to take care of yourself?"

Jack's first response was that he didn't have time to get regular exercise. He said he was too busy to take time off to run, walk, swim, or hike on a regular basis. He got some exercise working the farm, of course, but not enough to keep his weight below 210 pounds. He ate what he pleased, resisting his wife's regular pleas to lose weight. He liked eating meat every day and ate vegetables only under duress. He loved dessert and always had seconds if not thirds. Jack felt he exerted enough discipline at work; he didn't want to go home and watch what he ate or regulate how much he exercised.

When we asked what he did to manage his stress, he said he looked forward to dinner at the end of the day and the chance to watch TV with his kids. He said he "got things off his chest" by talking to his wife. Occasionally, he added, he took his dog for a walk at night, and he found that relaxing. While it's unlikely that Jack's lack of discipline *caused* either the diabetes or the arrhythmia, certainly his overeating, lack of exercise, and minimal stress management skills didn't *improve* those medical conditions. By eating poorly, not exercising, and failing to moderate his food intake, Jack missed his best chances to limit the damage his illnesses caused to his well-being. His stress management skills were poor enough that stress would remain a problem for him until he developed better strategies.

We confronted Jack with our observation that his primary stress management practice appeared to be complaining. We had listened to him gripe about this and that—weather, crops, employees, kids, and competition. We had listened to him complain about his wife and the demands of parenting. Now we put it on the line to Jack this way: "You're a sick man. You have two chronic illnesses that can and probably will get worse. While the way you live your life may not have caused your illnesses, changing your lifestyle could help you manage your illnesses and improve your health. You have some important lifestyle decisions to make."

We emphasized that if he wanted to improve his health, the complaining had to go. In order to optimize his chances of seeing his grandkids, he had to develop a stress management approach with more guts to it than mere complaining and self-pity. We introduced Jack to the LifeSkill of stopping what doesn't work. This LifeSkill is based upon one simple premise: Jack may not always know what to do to make each and every situation in his life perfect, but there are lots of things he can try.

In a broader context, each of us may not know what will work to make our lives run smoothly, but we can try out things and learn. At any given moment, we may not know how to manage our lives perfectly, but we can evaluate our actions and stop the ones that don't work. Jack may not have known how to influence the weather; he may not even have had all the information needed to eat properly or known how to manage his time well enough to fit exercise into his day. Those things were far less critical, though, than a sincere willingness to change habits that weren't working. Jack's coping repertoire lacked a willingness to evaluate what he was doing and a commitment to stop those actions that didn't serve him.

Another thing missing was an understanding that as long as he was doing things that didn't help his life, he would never learn what *would* work. That is, as long as he had too much dessert, ate red meat every day, and overate generally, he had no hope of improving his health through dietary change. As long as he continued to watch TV every evening and drive his car to the market, his chances of losing weight were slim. As long as he complained about the stress on his job rather than practicing essential LifeSkills, the likelihood of greater happiness and peace was nil.

Our direct message to Jack, and to *each* of our patients, is this: "You can alter the ways that you respond to difficult experiences!" For some sick people, the need to change habits is a must; if they fail to act, they will get sicker and possibly die. The LifeSkill of stopping what doesn't work takes it for granted that some things in life will be problematic and asks the question, Does how we respond make our lives worse or better? If what we do makes our experience worse, then a first step, and a *necessary* step, is to stop each and every action that isn't helping; we need to stop doing what doesn't work. It's only when we stop actions that *don't* help that we can come up with possibilities that *may*.

This LifeSkill reminds us that we have more control over our solutions to problems than we thought. Using this control is what making better, wiser choices is all about. Exercising positive control is at the heart of the Stress Free program. Once Jack grasped and accepted that concept, he felt empowered to make positive choices in his daily activities.

This LifeSkill takes perseverance. People have to keep practicing in order to strengthen their ability to respond in new and more positive ways. Jack had to choose to pay attention to what he was doing and ask himself what worked for him. When faced with the overwhelming circumstances of the bombing of London during World War II, Winston Churchill admonished, "Never give in, never give in, never,

never, never, never—in nothing, great or small, large or petty—never give in except to convictions of honor and good sense."

This LifeSkill puts front and center a focus on solutions, not problems. This emphasis is critically important. Too often individuals get so lost in the problem that they forget about potential solutions. Take Sandy, a grandmother who helped take care of her grandchildren. She was resentful of her children and dealt with that resentment by being crabby and acting like a martyr. This was an unconscious response. Until we pointed it out to her, she didn't recognize that crabbiness was her solution to her problem with her children. As solutions go, it was a failure; crabbiness didn't resolve Sandy's problem with her children or bring her happiness. We suggested that she give it up and try something else—in other words, that she stop doing what doesn't work.

Once Sandy acknowledged and relinquished her initial poor solution, she found that there were a variety of good solutions available to her. One better solution was to learn to talk more assertively to her children. Another was to practice belly-breathing to calm down. A third was to enlist the aid of her husband in the childcare. Too often people like Jack and Sandy are so concerned with a health issue or a problem at work or home that they forget how much flexibility they have. They get so lost in their problem that they forget the power of trying different solutions until they find one that works. They continue to practice what *doesn't* work and blame their continuing unhappiness and stress on the problem rather than seeing if their responses could be improved.

Because they don't even recognize their choices as a first step, they never get to evaluate the effectiveness of their coping strategies. People like Jack keep on doing the same destructive things over and over, which doesn't solve their problem. Jack continued to overeat, for example, when clearly that did his health and stress level no good. He continued to be too busy to exercise when regular exercise might have improved his diabetes. He was chronically stressed and yet continued to respond by complaining. He continued to use strategies that didn't work, and he wondered why his life and health were suffering. Jack was amazed when we asked him if his solutions worked, because he hadn't thought of his choices as solutions. He laughed, recognizing the absurdity, when we inquired as to whether extra desserts were a useful cure for diabetes.

We've used this LifeSkill often and have seen it work wonders with many of our patients. With some patients we've offered it as a stand-alone tool. Often, though, stopping what doesn't work is the gateway to other LifeSkills, such as belly-breathing and visualizing success.

Rebecca was an executive at a major financial services company. A vice-president, she had close to two hundred employees under her supervision. We saw her because of heart problems that had been exacerbated by the stock market slide. She was experiencing a business reversal for the first time in her succoooful career and was down on her abilities. This led to angina pain and high blood pressure.

Since the stock market slide that began in 2000, Rebecca's market group had done poorly; their sales were down almost 20 percent, and their profits were down even more. Being a competitive person, Rebecca took this business reversal personally. Therefore, she doubled her efforts and pushed her people harder. While that did little to increase her group's sales, it alienated her from her employees, making her stressed and angry. When we inquired about how she managed stress, Rebecca said that though she was too busy to meditate, which she believed would be useful, she went to the gym three times a week and had a good support network.

Rebecca was experiencing the effects of a particular form of stress known as job strain, and the consequences can be deadly. Job strain occurs when a person feels overwhelmed at work, as Rebecca (and so many of our clients) did. Rebecca started to lose her ability to manage the job demands effectively, which made her feel like a victim of her workload. We know from our research with Bank of America executives, and from the work of Dr. Redford Williams (a Duke Medical School cardiologist), that job strain creates anger, depression, hostility, anxiety, and isolation. It can lead to high blood pressure and enlargement of the left chamber of the heart. All the consequences of job strain are major risks for heart disease or even a heart attack. Rebecca was traveling down that road at a good clip, and it was lucky for her that she found us.

Listening to her, we discovered that Rebecca used comfort food as her primary stress management tool. She would
go home from work and unwind with something delicious to
eat. On the way home, she planned what would be on the
menu that evening. She often called her husband to discuss
which delicacy they would have for dinner that night. The
foods they chose were often expensive and/or fattening, and
they sometimes required extensive preparation. While they
provided Rebecca with some sense of comfort, they didn't
provide her with real strategies for dealing with stress and
problems at work.

As so many people do, Rebecca used food to manage her
painful emotions. She spent a good part of her spare time
reading about food and considered her daily treats the highlight of her day. She loved to eat and felt entitled to the good
feelings that food provided. While food is a wonderful pleasure, Rebecca used it instead of other, more successful strategies for comfort and stress management. Other people use
alcohol or cigarettes to reach the same goals. Food and drink
are wonderful gifts, among life's genuine delights, but they're
an ineffective way of coping with a stressful life.

When we determined that Rebecca's favored solution to
the problem of declining business was a focus on food, we
asked her if this solution solved her problem. Like Jack, she
hadn't considered her behavior an attempt at solution, but
after thinking for a moment she said that food *didn't* help; it

didn't actually calm her down or help her cope. In addition, eating never led to creative business thinking.

We told her that the two tests of any potential solution should be:

1. Does the solution (in her present case, eating rich or tasty foods) make you feel more peaceful or in control of your life?
2. Does the solution truly address the problem at hand?

When it was clear to Rebecca that her solution of eating didn't help her situation in any meaningful way, we asked her if she was willing to try something else. We reminded her that as long as she relied on food, her problems wouldn't go away, nor would she gain any new perspectives. We pointed out that as long as she relied on food, it was unlikely that other, possibly better solutions would be attempted. She agreed that it was silly to continue relying on strategies that had been declared ineffective.

A resourceful and courageous woman, Rebecca opted to stop doing what didn't work and try out other alternatives. Having acknowledged that her eating habits weren't working, and in fact were causing additional problems, she learned to appreciate many of the things in her life, including herself. She also learned to use food as an *occasional* reward rather than a daily treat.

We admired Rebecca for her efforts and willingness to change. She gave us a wonderful tag line that we in turn offer to you. She said that whenever she was tempted to return to old habits, she reminded herself, "Something that didn't work the first 100 times it was tried isn't likely to work the 101st time."

LifeSkill Exercise:
Stop Doing What Doesn't Work

Purpose

The purpose of this LifeSkill is . . .

- To learn to recognize when what you're doing is not successful and to stop.
- To learn to try new strategies that may have better results.

Practice

When faced with a difficult challenge:

1. Shift your attention fully to your belly.
2. Take at least two slow, deep breaths into and out of your belly.
3. Then fill your mind with an image of someone you love.
4. Hold the positive feelings that emerge in the area around your heart.
5. When calm ask yourself if the way you've handled the problem so far has worked.
6. If the answer is no, ask the relaxed part of you for a new solution to the problem.

Tips

- Feeling stressed isn't your major problem; it's your frustration over not knowing what will solve your difficulty.
- You will never know which solutions work if you keep repeating ones that don't.
- Have patience: it can take time to discover what is successful.
- Getting stressed over and over makes you feel helpless.
- Solutions that don't work add a second problem— a bad solution—to the first problem of a difficult situation.

Application

Use this LifeSkill . . .

- When you're frustrated.
- When you feel that you've tried everything.
- When you're bored with your life.
- When people say you need to change.
- When you're judging yourself harshly as a failure.
- When you have a bad habit.

"STOP DOING WHAT DOESN'T WORK" LIFESKILL:

When what you're doing isn't working, calm down and find a better solution.

CHAPTER 11

Just Say No

The phrase "Just Say No" was introduced in the 1980s as an admonition to resist illegal drugs. While the slogan proved to be too simplistic in addressing drug abuse in this country, the need to resist destructive behaviors is still critical to living a healthy, happy life. People need to be able to choose what they want to do, which implies rejecting that which they don't want to do. When they act in ways that go against what they think, feel, or want to do, stress and illness often result. A huge proportion of our patients are trapped in simple situations they want to get out of but can't, because they don't know how to say no.

Sally helped her brother-in-law, Stan, each week and hated it every single time. She hated it but said yes anyway, agreeing that he could leave his kids at her house for the day. Her sister, Alice, was married to a guy who would rather not watch his kids on his day off, and she felt helpless in the face of his disinterest. Stan worked for the post office and had Fridays off. On Saturdays, when he worked, Alice generally went over to Sally's house and they entertained their children together. *That* Sally looked forward to. But without fail, every single Friday morning Sally got a call from Stan, who would say hello, make some small talk, and then remind Sally of how much fun their kids had together. Since their kids did so well together, he'd say, could he drop them off while he did some some errands? Sally loved both of his children, and her sister was her best friend in the world. She would do anything to help them—just not every single Friday. And yet she just couldn't say no.

Helene worked for a large computer firm in Silicon Valley. She was the director of marketing and was quite successful in that role. However, she was constantly asked by her clients for favors and couldn't bring herself to refuse any reasonable request. So she got tickets to a ballgame for one client, responded to another by listening to his marital woes, helped still another by letting someone from his company shadow her, and even researched sales information for another. In each case, this was work that could have been done by the client's own staff, but people knew that Helene could always be counted on to go the extra mile. Though Helene was a generous and kind person, she felt taken advantage of—and she hated that feeling. But she just couldn't say no.

Donna had trouble saying no to her husband when he wanted to have sex with her. Donna and Sam had been married for eleven years, and they had two children. Their marriage worked pretty well for the most part; they liked each other and cooperated in raising their children. But Donna resented their sexual relationship and didn't know how to bring it up with her husband. When Donna and Sam first began sleeping together, Sam would sulk whenever Donna wasn't in the mood for sex. She couldn't resist his advances without his acting as if he was being unfairly punished. Over time Donna gave up trying to resist him and resigned herself to having sex whenever Sam desired. The only time she said no was when their children might see or hear them. Other than that, sex was his call. Donna loved her husband but resented his dominion over their sex life. She couldn't say no.

When we say yes but really mean no, it is analogous to driving a car with one foot on the gas and one foot on the brake. This conflict between what we say or do versus what we actually want to say or do creates a split between the mind and the body. That such a split causes stress and has been noted since Freud and confirmed by modern research.

A cartoon by Charles Schultz depicts this inner divide beautifully. Charlie Brown is sitting on the ground next to his football after failing to score a touchdown because he didn't have enough skill. He says to Lucy, "My mind and body hate each other." This is an example of the stress that results from thinking yes but saying no. But optimal performance can't result unless the mind and body are in harmony; unless saying yes means yes and saying no means no.

When you inhibit your true thoughts, feelings, or actions, this initiates a physical response that results in Type 2 stress. Under stress like this, the immune system does not work properly and there's an increase of stress hormones such as cortisol in the body. On the other side of the spectrum, when you acknowledge, express, and act upon your genuine thoughts and feelings, this congruence has positive benefits of equal weight. Lord Chesterfield expressed the intimate connection between mind and body in these words: "I find, by experience, that the mind and body are more than married, for they are most intimately united; and when one suffers, the other sympathizes."

This LifeSkill of saying no reminds our patients of two things that are easily forgotten. First, the earth won't fall out of its orbit if they refuse a request. Donna can say no if she doesn't want to have sex, and her husband will survive. Helene can say no if she doesn't wish to put herself out for every client, and she'd still be great at her job (though if her *biggest* client asks a favor and there's a huge deal in the works, she might want to hold off on starting her new quest for assertiveness). Likewise, Sally can say no to her brother-in-law and knows it won't be doomsday if he has to take care of his own children on his day off.

The second thing that this LifeSkill reminds us is that some ways of saying no work better than others. Becoming assertive means learning how to say no and express your needs and feelings *without* stepping on other people's feelings. Sally didn't have to scream at Stan that he was an inconsiderate jerk if she didn't want to watch his kids. Donna didn't have to tell Sam she hated him if he sulked when she wasn't in the mood. Helene could tell a client that she couldn't do what was requested without suggesting that the client was a pig for asking. Each of these women had both to learn that they could say no and to develop some simple strategies for doing so. The benefits of just saying no are enormous, as these women found; many stressful interactions can be avoided or minimized. As Sally, Donna, and Helene have discovered, when we don't assert ourselves the results are unwanted demands and increased stress.

Many people we work with have trouble being assertive with certain people or in certain situations. For example, Joan finds it next to impossible to say no to an invitation to a party, even though she definitely doesn't want to go. The result: she either goes and feel stressed before, during, and after, or she comes up with a last-minute excuse and feels guilty or concerned that she's harmed a friendship. Jack can't speak up to his boss when she hands him a task with an impossible deadline. The result: Jack feels stressed and over-loaded by his workload, angry at the unfairness of the situation, and worried about what his boss will say when he does not get the job done on time.

Almost any situation can lead to stress if you don't clearly state your opinion. Both work situations and personal relationships are made worse by swallowing your tongue. Consistently failing to express your thoughts and feelings can be destructive to the mind and body alike. In psychotherapy this is termed *suppression*, and it can be very damaging, as Dr. William Boyd, an eighteenth-century physician, warned: "The sorrow that hath no vent in tears may make other organs weep."

Not being honest about our needs and wants affects both patients and doctors alike. Jerome, a therapist we know, had a client named Jackie who always wanted a 6:00 p.m. appointment. Jackie came twice a week and on top of that regularly had emergencies. Each time there was a mini-crisis, she demanded to be seen that day—but she was free only during dinner, and that meant 6:00 p.m. That was supposed to be *home* time for Jerome. His wife worked all day too, and the couple shared child care and dinner preparation when they got home together after work. Still, more often than not, when Jackie told Jerome that he was the only one who could help her and that without his brilliance she would have a brutal evening, he relented and saw her at 6:00.

It wasn't that Jerome's wife gave him a hard time. She didn't. It wasn't that his children didn't get enough of his time. They did. It was just that when he arrived home at 7:30 p.m., his wife was exhausted, the kids were still in the bathtub and dinner still hadn't been happened. We reminded Jerome, who was a colleague of our and not a patient, of the ever-present opportunity to just say no when that was appropriate. By avoiding the stress of saying no to Jackie, Jerome created more stress in his life. By being nice, he set in motion a chain reaction that hurt other people and led to much more stress at home.

Donna was having sex out of obligation and fear of her husband's sullen response. Although her participation was voluntary, her assent was psychologically coerced, and coercion almost always brings resentment. Because resentment is a sign of powerlessness—we resent what we can't change—it usually hurts any relationship it's part of. Donna clearly resented Stan for forcing himself on her time and time again. Even though she said yes with her body, in her heart and soul she had no enthusiasm.

Helene said yes to clients she didn't want to say yes to out of a desire to be liked. She was afraid if she said no, she would be rejected. In other words, she used her yes (when she wanted to say no) to buy affection and support.

Sally said yes every week to Stan's request to drop off his kids, primarily as a kindness to her sister. Even though Sally had two kids of her own and a husband who traveled a lot, she took Stan's kids in because she didn't want to cause her sister stress. She was afraid that Stan would give Alice a hard time and that Alice would then have to bear more of the child care load. Sally was acting the concerned big sister, except they weren't eight and eleven anymore; they were thirty-two and thirty-five with families of their own. Sally said yes when she meant no, and added to her stress and made her more tired when her own husband came home.

Please understand: we're not suggesting that becoming assertive will be easy. As with each of the other LifeSkills, the skill of just saying no requires practice. If saying yes to things you don't want to do is a habit, then that habit will have to be changed. The only way to change a bad habit is by making a clear intention, rehearsing what you want to do differently, and then regularly practicing that new behavior. If you're accustomed to saying yes when you mean no, that old habit will initially remain easier than saying no when you mean no. There may be discomfort when you start this new habit—or *any* new habit. This is true even though you're switching to the healthy alternative of saying what you mean.

Something else that makes saying no harder than it needs to be is our concern that saying no is rude or selfish. We think that it's unseemly to state what we want or feel; we worry that our opinions and feelings don't count as much as those of other people around us. Many of us confuse stating what we want or don't want with being aggressive. It's not the same thing at all. Donna and Helene found out that being *assertive*—not *aggressive*—helped them feel better about how they dealt with people. They found that it raised their self esteem. Sally was surprised to discover, when she spoke honestly with her sister, that Alice felt the same way she did and thought that *Stan* was being rude. In fact, Alice had been wondering to herself why Sally took her kids in each and every week. The only information she had gotten from Sam was that Sally likes the kids so much (and the cousins got along so well) that Sally *wanted* to have them over. Alice, glad to have an arrangement that made her busy life run more smoothly, had never asked Sally if it was really okay.

Remember, though, that just saying no is no guarantee that you'll get what you want or that things will turn out fine.

It does not *guarantee* success, but it gives you the best chance of it. When you say no to what you don't want to do, then you're able to strongly assert yes when you agree. Even after Sally and Alice talked, there were many weeks when Sally gladly took the kids in. However, she took them when she wanted to and therefore did so without resentment. Even after Helene mastered the LifeSkill of saying no, there were many times when she was happy to help her clients with something extra. She liked many of them and was glad to extend herself on their behalf. However, she could choose when those times would be and not resent her clients for asking. Finally, Donna wanted an active sex life; she simply wanted a voice in how and when. When she learned to say no to Stan when her heart wasn't in it, their lovemaking became a little less frequent but a lot more passionate. Now when Donna said yes, she meant it.

There are three things that make learning to say no more effective:

1. Be aware of when saying no is appropriate.
2. Know the difference between being assertive, being non-assertive, and being aggressive.
3. Practice saying no in simple, nonthreatening situations first, and then move on to bigger challenges.

Let's look at each of these in a little more detail. First, say no only in appropriate situations—that is, when you actually have a choice. If you say no to paying your taxes, you're breaking the law. If you say no to stopping at a red light, you're inviting a ticket. If you have to finish a vital report that requires you to stay at the office late one day, saying no may not be the best option. But if such deadlines happen every week, you have the choice as to whether or not you wish to remain employed at that company. Don't blame your boss for asking you to do something you don't want to do; that's not appropriate. He has a right to ask, and you have a right to say no. Learn to say no when the choice is clearly yours.

Saying no when appropriate means it's okay for you to put yourself first. You don't always have to go to the back of the line or take the smallest portion. You have the right to be treated with respect, to be listened to and taken seriously. You also have the right to say no and not feel guilty. If someone else feels bad because you refuse them something, that's their choice of reaction; it's not necessarily your doing. However, saying no appropriately implies that you have examined the consequences of your actions. Don't say no simply out of spite. Examine the situation before deciding to offer your opinion. You don't have to say no any more than you have to say yes. You can decide on a case-by-case basis.

The second tool that will help you say no more effectively is knowing the difference between being assertive, being nonassertive, and being aggressive. Being assertive means standing up for your rights, expressing your opinions, and sharing your feelings in direct, honest, and appropriate communication. You can say no without being unkind. In fact, you *must*. But just as it isn't right for other poeple to boss you around, it isn't right for you to boss other people around.

You're being aggressive, not assertive, when you violate other people's rights in standing up for your own. The same goes for ignoring or dismissing the wants, opinions, and feelings of others.

Being nonassertive means saying yes when you want to say no and say no when you want to say yes. It means feeling guilty when you turn people down, and believing that their needs are more important than your own. Being nonassertive is going along to get along—even when you don't want to. When you're assertive, you can say yes or no depending on the situation and your experience. When you're nonassertive, you say yes because someone else wants you to. Donna was nonassertive with her husband, and Sally was nonassertive with her brother-in-law, and Helene was nonassertive with her clients. They were each nonassertive in a situation where they had a legitimate choice and where saying either yes or no was appropriate.

The third tool is our old standby: practice. There are a number of ways to practice the skill of just saying no. If you have some warning (as Sally did every week), you can think of the most direct response ahead of time; you can visualize what you want to say and picture yourself saying it kindly but firmly, or you can write down what you want to say. There's a growing body of research that indicates that the ability to express feelings, especially in writing, is of great benefit and improves the health of both mind and body. Consider the following positive benefits. One study found that people who wrote down and rehearsed a new, more positive response to a stressful situation had an improvement in memory and experienced more happiness. In addition a group of senior-level engineers who were encouraged to express their fears and other true feelings after being laid off found new jobs more quickly than those who denied the impact.

Trying out saying no with a friend in a role-playing situation is an ideal way to begin practicing this LifeSkill. Your friend can pretend to be a person you're having trouble with, and you can practice being assertive until it starts to feel natural. When you've reached that point, practice saying no to people with whom you feel comfortable enough to assert yourself. Finally, confront the troublesome situations in your life directly when they occur. When you do so appropriately and with assertion, remembering that you own both your yes and your no, you will reduce your stress, increase your self esteem, and become more confident.

It's our hope that one day we can all be as clear, assertive, and direct in our communication as Sister Mary Katherine, who entered the Monastery of Silence as a young woman.

The priest who admitted her said, "Sister, this is a silent

monastery. You're welcome here as long as you like, but you may not speak until I direct you to do so."

Sister Mary Katherine lived in the monastery for five years before the priest said to her, "Sister Mary Katherine, now that you've been here for five years, you may speak two words."

Sister Mary Katherine said, "Hard bed."

"I'm sorry to hear that," the priest said, "We'll get you a better bed."

After another five years, the priest called Sister Mary Katherine to him and said, "You may say another two words, Sister."

"Cold food," said Sister Mary Katherine. Shaking his head apologetically, the priest assured her that the food would be better in the future.

On her fifteenth anniversary at the monastery, the priest again called Sister Mary Katherine into his office. "You may say two words today," he said.

"I quit," said Sister Mary Katherine.

"It's probably best," replied the priest. "You've done nothing but bitch since you got here."

LifeSkill Exercise:
Just Say No

Purpose

The purpose of this LifeSkill is . . .

- To remind you that you have choices, including the option of saying no.
- To highlight the fact that, because you *can* say no, your yes is real and not forced.
- To remind you that you're responsible for the choices you make (and to make them wisely).

Practice

When someone asks you to do something you know you don't want to do:

1. Take two or three slow, deep belly-breaths.
2. Then say, "I need a few moments to think about this. Can I get back to you in a little while?"
3. When you offer your response, choose one of the following: "I've thought about this, and unfortunately I'm not going to be able to help you out this time. I realize this may be disappointing to you, but it's what I've decided"; or, "I'm not going to be able to help you out

in the way you asked; maybe together we can come up
with a solution that works for us both."

Tips

- At first, practice saying no with people you trust,
  knowing that they will respond well.
- Remember that you can choose to say no. Give the
  answer you *want* to give.
- You don't have to do something just because someone
  asks you to.
- If you're not sure what answer you want to give, always
  ask for time to think over the request.
- You don't have to say no any more than you have to
  say yes; the choice is always yours.

Application

Use this LifeSkill . . .

- When you're asked to take on extra work.
- When you're asked to help out over and over in your
  family.
- When you need to resist the bad habits of peers.
- When salespeople are pushing you to buy something
  you do not need.

- When a friend wants you to come over and you're exhausted.

"JUST SAY NO" LIFESKILL:

Just saying no is a way of setting limits, being assertive without being angry, and communicating what you do and don't want to do to yourself and to others.

CHAPTER 12

Accept What You Cannot Change

Our final LifeSkill, accept what you cannot change, uses the Serenity Prayer as its foundation. This prayer, central to the 12-step programs, is a simple way of reminding all of us that finding inner peace is a necessary and ongoing part of the human quest. Life can be hard at times, and sometimes there's nothing we can do to alter the way things turn out. Many of us have had very difficult experiences that we've had to make peace with.

James had been hit by a car and came to us while he was suffering from the subsequent chronic pain. James was only twenty-two and had been a star player on his college volleyball team. In fact, he'd been a stellar athlete for as long as he could remember. After the tragic car accident that broke his pelvis and shattered two of the vertebrae in his back, James suffered from periods of excruciating pain that medication couldn't ease, as well as from depression, why-me rage, and helplessness. He couldn't understand how such a devastating loss could occur to someone so young and healthy.

Dorothy slipped and fell just outside her office building one icy day. She (and the purse and computer she was carrying) went crashing to the ground with such force that she broke her ankle in three places. Dorothy was forty years old at the time—a wife, parent, and full-time stockbroker. We saw her some months later, when she was recuperating from the trauma and in significant pain.

Francine's husband had moved away a couple of years earlier, refusing to pay child support, and couldn't be contacted. At age thirty-eight, she was left with two children to parent alone, with neither husband nor financial support forthcoming. In major financial trouble and stressed out of her mind, Francine developed neck and back problems. Every time her body hurt, she cursed her husband once again. He was literally a pain in the neck for her, even though he had been absent for more than two years.

Each of these people experienced a high level of stress but also felt an added torment from their sense that life hadn't been fair. James was outraged that a devastating accident could happen to someone so young. Dorothy claimed negligence on the part of her employer, though it was simply the sort of cold and icy day on which accidents happen. Francine felt betrayed by a man who had promised his life to her and then just took off. When they came to see us, none of these people could contemplate the power of acceptance—that is, the power of making peace with what they couldn't change. This inability only exacerbated their pain and suffering.

Each of these individuals had heard of the Serenity Prayer, which calls people to distinguish between things and events they can change and those they cannot. We teach it to people because it serves as a gentle reminder that human beings aren't always in charge. Things happen that we wish had *not* happened. Life is often unpredictable and painful. People change, move, act selfishly, and fail. We don't always know how things will work out, and too often when things *don't* go the way we hope we react with anger and outrage. The Serenity Prayer highlights a LifeSkill that's central to our Stress Free program: the wisdom to know when to argue and when to accept.

What strikes us is how few people practice this wise and timeless message. The Serenity Prayer's expression of the limits of human control is gentle, yet powerful—so powerful that it dictates human happiness. There are many things outside our control. James couldn't control the car that hit him. Dorothy couldn't control the weather. Francine couldn't control the affections or location of her ex-husband. In response to difficulties like these, the perennial wisdom of the Serenity Prayer says,

> *Grant me the serenity to accept the things I cannot*
> * change,*
> *The courage to change the things I can,*
> *And the wisdom to know the difference.*

This is a simple but profoundly wise prayer. Not heeding its message caused James, Francine, and Dorothy extra and unnecessary suffering. Perhaps you, too, need to work on accepting certain things as they are.

At the heart of this LifeSkill is the challenge to make things better when you can but also to recognize those times when you don't have the power to change reality. For some people, the Serenity Prayer is about surrendering to a higher power. People who are religious see in their acceptance of the unchangeable a surrender to God. This allows them to reconnect to their spiritual support in a time of difficulty. This perspective isn't religious per se, however. Although it touches on questions of spirituality and ultimate belief, even an agnostic or an atheist can perceive a higher power, perhaps in terms of the laws of science or in the form of ethical codes of behavior. Whatever the form of the belief, it's not as important as the acknowledgment that ultimately we must accept that which we cannot control.

James was going to have to accept that his athletic career was over; he wouldn't be playing volleyball again for a top collegiate program. His loss was painful and sad, and it was final. Dorothy was going to have to accept that mistakes happen and that it's often no one's fault. There was no one she could blame for her pain or for the upheaval in her life. Francine was going to have to accept that some marriages end and not all marital partners are reliable or trustworthy. Her loss of faith was deep, and the economic and familial disruption would have lasting repercussions for herself and her children.

The question we posed to each of these people when they came to us for advice concerned the wisdom of continually struggling with something that can't be undone. We inquired of each of them whether it helped their lives to argue with the cards they were dealt. Could the accident or the fall or the disappearance of the husband be undone? Could the reality of their lives be changed? Each of them said no. They understood that nothing could alter the specific event that caused them distress. They glimpsed the understanding that the past is immutable, but present-day perceptions and approaches can be altered.

In talking to James, Dorothy, and Francine, we were mindful of the need for grieving. We understood the importance of expressing their feelings—in particular, feelings of loss, outrage, and sadness. When things go wrong, people feel pain; this is normal. People need to take time to process any loss, and part of that process is expressing negative emotions. Even as we teach the LifeSkill of acceptance, we remind all our patients that expressing painful feelings is important and even necessary as they heal from their grief.

One of the ways we introduced this LifeSkill to James was through the analogy of being stuck in a brutal traffic jam—a traffic jam from hell. (Working in the San Francisco Bay Area, we use congested traffic as an exemplar of many difficult stresses.) We asked James if he had ever been in a traffic jam caused by an accident. He said, "Of course." We asked him to join us in imagining a doozy of a traffic jam. Picture this, we said:

Imagine that you're on the freeway about three miles south of San Francisco. You're abruptly forced to slow down and then stop because the cars up ahead stop. Now there's no movement in sight. You're in the middle lane, and it's still a couple of miles to the next exit. To make things worse, you have an important appointment in twenty minutes, for which you're already running late. Worse still, it's hot outside, and the air pollution is high.

This is clearly not a pleasant experience. It's worse only for the people in the accident that you suspect lies ahead, or for anyone who has a real emergency and can't get out of line. You and a host of other drivers are stuck, inconvenienced, late for appointments of varying kinds, hot, and tired.

The question we posed to James was, "Is the situation described above one you could quickly change?" He answered no. Next we asked, "Stuck in traffic as the scenario suggests, is there anything you would have control over?" "Nothing," he answered. We pressed him: "Nothing at *all*?" He then added, "Except maybe how upset you get."

If you can't control the traffic but you can control yourself, how do you spend your time stuck in the car? Do you rant and rave about how unfair the traffic jam is? Do you feel sorry for yourself? Do you complain about the terrible drivers who cause accidents and stall traffic? Do you talk about how awful it is to live in such a crowded area? Do you simply sit and fume? In reality, of course, people stuck in traffic might give a resounding yes to *all* of these questions. But are these reactions *helpful*?

That's what we asked James in teaching this new LifeSkill. Would any of these responses help your mood or the traffic? It was obvious that they would do neither.

So what then *do* you do? What's the best response when you can't control the traffic but have some control over how upset you get? James suggested that he might take a nap to get through the delay. Other possibilities include getting some work done, people-watching, or counting your blessings. Since there was nothing he could do to get the road cleared, James had to focus his attention on aspects of the situation that he had influence upon. The word that came to his lips after thinking about this for a while was *choices*; he had *choices*. In a stressful situation like a traffic jam, he could choose the most helpful available alternative.

After completing this exercise, we suggested to James that his accident wasn't that different from being stuck in traffic. The accident was certainly more painful, and it clearly made much more of an impact on his life, leaving him with chronic pain and preventing him from competing in volleyball. The imaginary traffic jam was nothing compared to the damage James had suffered from his accident. But in the essential experience of being stuck without a tangible way out, was it any different? James could no more easily erase the pain in his body than he could magically fly above the traffic.

With the help of his new LifeSkill, James learned to make better choices. He volunteered to teach children volleyball, learned tools (including other LifeSkills) that helped him deal with the pain, and started therapy. Our work with James led him to the understanding that when he's stuck in situations such as traffic jams or painful life experiences, it's important to recognize that he has choices in the way he reacts.

We've found the LifeSkill of acceptance helpful in assisting our clients to make peace with events from the past that can't be altered. James's accident had occurred more than two years before we saw him. Dorothy had slipped and fallen ten months before her visit to us, and Francine's husband had been gone for almost three years. If there's one thing that never changes, no matter how hard we push or how much courage we put into trying to change things, it's the past. The past is *done*. How each of the people profiled in this chapter related to what happened to them could be changed, though the initial happening could not. One of life's most difficult lessons is accepting that nothing that occurred even as short a time ago as this morning can be altered. The Serenity Prayer is a wonderful tool for making peace with reality and has saved many of our patients from much needless suffering.

Another life difficulty where the Serenity Prayer works well is with struggles with family members and other people to whom we're close. Tom is a perfect example. He was a forty-five-year-old heart patient who complained a lot about his wife. They had been married for twenty years, had three kids, and owned a nice home. Yet Tom struggled to accept several of his wife's habits—in particular, her need for order in everything from emotions to where the paper towels were kept. She liked the house neat, with everything in its place. Tom, on the other hand, took a more casual approach.

Tom spent time each day trying to change his wife, Sonya, and after two decades he was still unsuccessful. She rejected all his offers of friendly advice. Each time Sonya behaved in the orderly way she always behaved, Tom felt rejected and unhappy. What he didn't realize was that his mission to change his wife, rather than himself, was doomed to failure from the start. When we saw Tom, it was clear (to him as well as to us) that his desire to change Sonya wasn't working out well.

Most of us don't like to be told how to do things differently. We prefer to muddle along in our old ways rather than listen to new ideas. Often we don't see even genuinely good advice as helpful, condemning it as annoying or intrusive. Advice from family members and friends is typically even less welcome than advice from strangers (such as therapists).

Though we don't like to receive advice ourselves, we expect others to welcome it. Likewise, the same people who don't listen to us are often first in line to offer us their opinions. Take Tom and Sonya: Tom got frustrated when Sonya wouldn't listen to his suggestions for improvement, but he didn't listen to her either. When the couple finally talked frankly about this issue, it turned out Sonya wasn't happy with Tom's pushiness; she reported with gusto how little he listened to her litany of complaints. Sonya felt frustrated that he was always on her case, always trying to change her. She was happy with her life, apart from Tom's pestering. She had quickly grown to recognize that look on his face that heralded a talking-to, and she'd tell him to "take his opinions and shove them."

We talked to Tom about how frustrated he got because his wife wouldn't change, and about how much energy he wasted in his attempts at reform. We asked him, "How does it feel knowing that you have no power to make your wife change?" He said it felt awful. He was always out of control, and their relationship suffered. We then asked him if he knew the Serenity Prayer. He said yes, and then we wondered aloud if this was a situation best suited for courage or acceptance. Tom said, "I've had all the courage in the world, and none of the acceptance." We asked him to reflect upon where wisdom might lie in this situation. As he did so, he calmed down. He said, "Wisdom clearly says that Sonya isn't going to change unless she chooses to." With this understanding, he got a glimpse of the power of accepting what he couldn't change, and he started to make realistic plans to improve their marriage.

It was clear to us that Sonya would do whatever she pleased, as she had been doing for the past twenty years. As two decades of marriage had shown Tom, his wife was a stubborn woman. However, from our perspective, we could clearly see how alike they both were. Tom was an equally stubborn man. His suffering had been intensified because he'd tried to force change where acceptance might have led to peace and a more satisfying marriage.

As Tom grew in his understanding of accepting what he could not change, his attitude toward his wife improved. He saw the clear benefits of her differing style of house and life management and was able to value her good points. He and his wife spent a short but productive period of time going to couple's therapy. The first time they'd tried this, some years back, it was a failure, because each tried to prove the other wrong. This time the therapy facilitated the discovery of places of accommodation so that they could more easily live together. Tom realized that when you live with someone, that person has as much right to her choices as you have to yours. As his hostility and resentment lessened, his marriage improved—and not coincidentally, so did his blood pressure.

Even with the daunting task of coping with the death of a relative or friend, the skill of accepting what you cannot change is of great benefit. One patient of ours, Leslie, had a child that she and her husband loved dearly. Theirs was a close family, and both parents spent a lot of time with David. Leslie had her own custom printing business, and she and David assumed that he would take over the family business when he was old enough. One morning David woke up complaining of an excruciating headache. When he was rushed to the hospital, the diagnosis was that he was suffering from an inoperable brain tumor that was growing rapidly.

This dreadful news was devastating to the family, and we counseled them on trying to adapt to the reality of the situation. When something awful like this happens, making peace is extremely painful. But over time most people understand that death is a part of life and can't be changed.

One of David's family's favorite shared recreations was sailing; they all felt at home at sea. In the course of our meetings with them, they repeated to us a Celtic blessing used by ancient sailors. They used this blessing to help them cope and come to some peace.

> *Deep peace of the running wave to you.*
> *Deep peace of the flowing air to you.*
> *Deep peace of the quiet air to you.*
> *Deep peace of the shining stars to you.*
> *Deep peace of the gentle night to you.*
> *Moon and stars pour their healing light on you.*
> *Deep peace to you.*

When David died three weeks later, this prayerful expression of serenity was recited by both his parents as his epitaph. They used peace to begin their grieving process and in time surmounted the greatest test of their serenity. Fortunately, for most of us our tests are simpler. But whether what we face is large (as in a child's death) or small (as in different levels of marital cleanliness), everyone can benefit from the Serenity Prayer's reminder to accept what cannot be changed and work hard to change what we can.

LifeSkill Exercise:
Accept What You Cannot Change

Purpose

The purpose of this LifeSkill is . . .

- To learn to choose battles you have a chance of win-
  ning.
- To learn to practice peacefulness whenever you can.
- To learn to accept things you cannot change.

Practice

If you feel controlled by your circumstances in a particular
situation—a traffic jam, for example, or by a life-threatening
disease—it's important to assess whether you have alternatives (such as a different route or an alternative therapy) or
whether there's nothing you can do to alter the circumstances. If the latter, you need the serenity to accept that you
can do nothing to change your situation.

Try the following to help yourself achieve that serenity:

1. Take two slow, deep belly-breaths and think of something beautiful in your life.
2. Remind yourself that to solve the problem you need
   serenity and wisdom, not anger or despair.

3. Ask yourself, "If I can't change this situation, what can I do to make peace with it?"

4. Fully accept your life in body, mind, and spirit.

Tips

- Trying to change a situation that isn't in your control leads to frustration.
- When you feel frustrated and continue to argue with things that can't be changed, you feel helpless and angry.
- Your mind and body suffer when you get angry.
- Feeling less frustration allows you to focus on the things you do that might make a difference—if not to the circumstances, then at least to your response.

Application

Use this LifeSkill . . .

- When you find yourself getting frustrated by a situation that won't go away.
- When you find yourself getting frustrated by a friend's or family member's irritating behavior.
- When you have a financial setback.
- When you don't get the promotion you feel you deserve.
- When you're trying to cope with a chronic illness.

- When you're experiencing changed circumstances, such as retirement or a move.
- When someone you love dies.

"ACCEPT WHAT YOU CANNOT CHANGE" LIFESKILL:

In the words of the Serenity Prayer, "Grant me the serenity to accept the things I cannot change, the courage to change the things I can, and the wisdom to know the difference."

CHAPTER 13

No Time Like the Present

We have introduced you to the Stress Free program containing ten powerful skills that will change the way you live your life. We have shared with you stories of people for whom each of the LifeSkills have been helpful. The specific LifeSkills range from the simplest (breathe from your belly) to more complex (just say no). There are ten distinct LifeSkills, but the bottom line is simple: "All roads lead to Rome." In other words, all the LifeSkills stop stress. All the LifeSkills make you healthier and happier.

The program works whether you start with the skill most germane to the problems you face or the first skill we offer. Once you learn one, it becomes easier to learn and implement the others. As with a box of tools, the more skills you have, the greater the ability to handle any of life's difficult situations. With LifeSkills in your toolbox, you have the power to create greater happiness, increased fulfillment, and optimal health. So we remind you and exhort you to . . . start with any LifeSkill, but start *now*. Each LifeSkill takes about ten minutes to learn. Think about how little time that is. That's about the amount of time we spend each day in the shower, or dressing and tying our shoes, or brushing our teeth and hair.

You may think that sounds overly optimistic, but our research and our clinical practice confirm that these LifeSkills can be learned in ten minutes—and that they *work*. Once learned, each LifeSkill takes a minute to as little as fifteen seconds to practice. Most important, as you practice, your mind and body will feel positive results in about six to ten seconds.

The LifeSkills that offer the most immediate benefit are the two dealing with appreciation—appreciating other people and life itself, and appreciating yourself (where you focus on the good that you do). The many aspects of the power of appreciation work to reduce stress and increase happiness almost instantly. Think about it. You can get immediate results from very brief practice. You can feel better almost instantly, no matter where you are or what you're doing. Remember our mantra: ten minutes to learn, a minute to practice, and a powerful result in ten seconds. There's almost nothing else you will ever learn that offers such bang for your buck and is so important for the health of your body, mind, and relationships.

Each of the LifeSkills in the Stress Free program is deceptively simple but amazingly powerful. They have been proven to work in our research and in our clinical practice with many people tackling a wide array of problems. These skills have

been used by people all over the world to reduce their suffering and improve their health. Remember, though, that reading this book is only the beginning. Passively reading the
book starts to give you the results you deserve and want, but
you have to practice and apply the specific skills to your life
to get the full benefit.

Reading a diet book won't result in weight loss; reading a
DMV manual on rules of the road won't teach you how to
drive; and watching an exercise video won't make you fit.
Likewise, just reading this book isn't enough. It's a good
beginning, though. We've found that people get some benefit
immediately because the LifeSkills are so simple and easy to
understand.

In order to change your experience of stress and increase
your happiness, you need to use the LifeSkills regularly. We
have shown you, through the lives of people we've worked
with, how quickly the skills work and how they benefit both
mind and body. We cannot stress enough, though, the fact
that to fully benefit, you need to *practice* the LifeSkills. You
need to belly-breathe and visualize success and just say no
when appropriate.

Remember to practice belly-breathing when you're under
stress and you need to calm down. Try practicing self appreciation when you're in a good mood and want to make a nice
moment better. Cultivate appreciation when you're feeling
overwhelmed: the few moments spent really noticing the colors of a beautiful sunset or allowing your child to melt your

heart will revive you. When it's hard to see what path to take, visualize success and experience the gift of seeing that a good outcome is possible. Learn to just say no, when appropriate, to reduce stress and assert the value of *you*. Practice tensing to relax as a means to calm yourself in the most difficult of situations. Work hard to improve your lot but accept what you cannot change, and you cement the underpinning of good mental health.

There's a wonderful story involving the meditation teacher Ram Dass that we like to tell about the importance of regular practice. After one of his lectures in New York, a woman from the audience asked Ram Dass how much he meditated each day. He responded, "Three minutes." There was an audible gasp of disbelief from the entire audience. Three minutes, and you're a famous meditation teacher? With a smile, Ram Dass said, "Yes, I meditate every single day for three minutes, which is much better than not meditating every day for thirty minutes!"

If you've already started to practice these LifeSkills, you know that they work. You know the power of these simple strategies. Enjoy working with the Stress Free program and watch yourself, moment by moment, create a better life. A few minutes of peace, a moment of appreciation, the ability to see good things in the future—these are your goal and your reward. The experience of peace, calm, and appreciation often leads to better health, reduced tension and muscle pain, and fewer headaches. What emerges with regular practice is the elusive moment-to-moment happiness—something we all deserve.

It has often been said that the journey, not the destination, is what counts. That journey is your life. LifeSkills aren't just another item on your to-do list. These essential strategies will change the lens through which you view your life. For most people, that lens becomes more clear the longer they practice, and with a clear lens life's beauty emerges. Stress Free living, happiness, and fewer aches and pains are the result.

Long-term practice of some or all of the LifeSkills enhances the results of your *daily* practice and helps create optimal physical health. When you practice a LifeSkill, improvement begins immediately. But it can often take between ten and twelve weeks to uncover a dysfunctional way of seeing/thinking/behaving and replace it with a new approach. We arrived at this ten-to-twelve-week timetable after looking at the current scientific understanding of basic brain and nervous system functioning. This timetable has been shown to be accurate when tracking physical fitness, the effects of psychotherapy, dieting, playing a musical instrument, developing an athletic skill, and virtually every aspect of life where learning a new skill is required. So practice, enjoy the boost you get every time you practice, and be patient as long-term changes unfold.

Perhaps one of the most profound lessons that unfolds from working with the Stress Free program is that to a large degree you create how the world appears. You can't control the weather, international events, the roller-coaster of the stock market, the misbehavior of your children, the demands of your work, or the inevitable declines of aging. But you *can* change your reaction to those life events.

The choices you make go a long way toward creating the quality of your life. One way to respond to life is through withdrawal, stubbornness, bitterness, and/or helplessness. By contrast, we can choose to appreciate and respond to the inevitable challenges we all face. LifeSkills are the tools with which to take control of your life. We have seen scores of suffering people and understand that life is difficult, health is precarious, and people can be unreliable. Patients remind us every day that change and transition are painful and that things go wrong. Even though all these things are true, it's important to remember that you always have a choice about how to respond.

You largely determine what impact the events of your life will have on your experience, and you always have some choice. There's a wonderful quip by Mae West, who in 1938 said, "When I have to choose between two evils, I always choose the one I have not tried before." Generally speaking, you can react either as a victim or as an active creator of a more positive experience. We want you to choose to be a creator. We want you to choose happiness and well-being. We want you to join the thousands of people who have benefited from the Stress Free program. We want you to have better health, more happiness, and improved performance. This message of the power of choice is consistent with every form of meditation and prayer that has emerged from the world's spiritual teachings since the beginning of time.

If you're already using LifeSkills, you may wonder how you will know whether a given LifeSkill is working. Many people have shared with us signposts that appear as LifeSkills take effect. First, you notice that it becomes easier to remember and use whatever LifeSkill you're working with; in effect, the new skill becomes a habit, and you use it with increasing ease and flexibility. When you practice a LifeSkill such as belly-breathing, you notice that the inner sense of balance, stillness, and equanimity lasts for a longer time. Finally, you notice that the peace you experience becomes deeper. You spend more and more time in your optimal performance zone.

As this happens, you recognize that you don't lose your inner balance as easily. When you're cut off in traffic, receive good or bad news about a stock that you own or your child's grades on a report card, or have to work late under a pressing deadline, you stay more centered. This is not to say that you become indifferent or passive, but that because of practice you know you can deal with difficult situations. As you see that you can deal successfully with challenges and stay calm, negative experiences hold less power.

Between the first practice of a LifeSkill and long-term positive results, patients report a shift from *believing* that they can use LifeSkills to create a more fulfilling life to *knowing* that they can. Our successful patients display a confidence that no one can take from them. They feel good, and they *know* they feel good. They also know their success comes from their effort and not luck or chance.

In a famous BBC television interview with Dr. Carl Jung toward the end of his life, the interviewer asked Jung if, as a scientist and psychiatrist who explored the depths of the mind, he believed in God. In the film, Jung leans forward, peers intently over his glasses, and states very firmly and clearly, "I do not believe . . . I know!" His life experience and practice had transformed a belief into a certainty. This certainty of success is our ultimate goal. It's the goal for you, for all of our patients, and for us as well.

You can start using LifeSkills no matter where you are in your life. You're never too old or too young. There's a well-known expression that says, "Life is what happens while you're busy making other plans." Don't let life get away from you: use what you've learned in this book and take charge of your life. With practice, making better, more positive decisions, both at work and at home, will become normal. This isn't an abstract idea but the reality of knowing that you have the power to control your stress, look for the good in your life, and make better choices at any time.

Last but not least, LifeSkills provide a foundation for change that you can use as a stepping-stone for other life-affirming changes. As you've seen from the stories in this book, the Stress Free program has helped our patients improve their diet, exercise, and career; enabled the proper use of medications; improved communication and relationships; and, of course, reduced stress. Each skill provides the calm and the inner balance required for making any lasting life changes. That peace and calm help you realize that this truly is the first day of the rest of your life and that you can make a fresh start toward greater health and happiness. All you need is the tools in this book and a willingness to practice!

Afterword

All you need to do is work with the Stress Free program as Margaret did, and positive results will follow. Margaret is a perfect example of someone who successfully completed the Stress Free program. We use Margaret's story here to highlight the central points of this book: practice wherever you can, practice often, have patience, and remember that LifeSkills take only a few minutes of your day and that the Stress Free program works on both your body and your mind. We also tell Margaret's story because from the beginning, her success was far from assured. We worked with Margaret extensively to help her break the habit of nonstop rushing and thus free herself from the resulting stress and pain.

When we met Margaret, she was exhausted but appeared to suffer from nothing more than an overloaded lifestyle. We soon learned that Margaret's hectic day-to-day life was a problem. Her too-busy schedule left her with not enough rest and with chronic back pain. She did not set aside enough time to spend with her husband, and her married life had quickly become unfulfilled. Margaret's kids felt like a burden to her, and the lack of rest gave her a short fuse. To cut to the chase: Margaret was stressed out and at the end of her rope.

At our first meeting, we taught Margaret two LifeSkills: Slow Down, and Appreciation. We guided her in both practices and discussed the ways in which she could use those skills in her life. We then made an appointment to see her in two weeks and sent her home. Margaret went home and promptly forgot to practice. When she returned in two weeks, she informed us that the Stress Free program did not work and that there was little reason for her to make any further appointments.

When we asked her about the two weeks between visits, we found out that by the time she had reached the hospital parking lot, Margaret was back in overdrive. She reminded herself of her inexhaustible list of chores and her resentment toward her husband for not pitching in. Within about ten minutes, the idea of slowing down felt like a burden. She felt that she had nothing to appreciate. By the time she got home, our visit was a memory and her back throbbed.

During the second visit, we guided Margaret in the simple but powerful exercise of walking more slowly. We slowly wandered the halls of the hospital, chatting about appreciating her legs and the fact that they moved. We chatted about her lovely children. And every time she sped up either her walking or her talking, we simply asked her to take a deep breath. As she was breathing, we reminded her that many people in the hospital would be happy to exchange their sick lives for her busy one.

At the debriefing session that followed, Margaret burst

into tears. She said she could not imagine that her husband, friends, children, and coworkers could ever tolerate her taking any time for herself. We got a glimpse into the incredible pressure she was under and how little room she felt she had to be herself. We explained a bit about how Type 2 stress makes you feel that you are always under the gun, and we offered sympathy for the demands she faced. We also asked her, at the end of the appreciative slow walking, if her back felt less tight, and she said yes.

Considering how quickly Margaret forgot the lessons of our first visit, we asked her to do two things for us: First, we asked her to, as she left the hospital, slow down and appreciate the beauty of the day, and to, once her car started, give thanks for her good fortune. Second, we asked her to e-mail us every thirty-six hours with a list of things she had appreciated. At first her appreciation lists were short, but as time went on they got a little more detailed. Margaret began to take a moment as she entered the supermarket to marvel at the enormous choice of foods. She began to catch herself as she was hurrying, and she began to walk with patience a few moments at a time. She started to breathe deeply and appreciate the sunshine that was available almost every day. She regularly thanked her friends for their attention. She saw how lucky she was to have a safe house in a safe neighborhood in a free country. Most important, she started to notice the enormous demands on her husband and the effort he put out for their family.

The thing Margaret learned that she found most helpful was that rushing usually did not make her more productive. Slowing down when walking, paying attention when driving, and eating her food with concentration actually gave her more energy. She saw that walking slowly allowed her to see the beauty all around her, that driving with more attention reduced stress, and that eating with concentration allowed the taste of the food to emerge. During our third visit, Margaret was describing her success and expressing dissatisfaction with the pace of change. Her back ached less but still hurt, and she still felt she did not have enough time. We laughed to ourselves: here was a woman so in a hurry that slowing down had to be accomplished overnight.

We reminded Margaret that practice takes time. It takes time to learn to rush, rush, rush—and it takes time to slow down, pay attention, and smell the roses. When she left the session this time, we gave Margaret another assignment: to tell her husband, at the end of every day, something she had done with slow and deep attention, and something she had appreciated. We were delighted to hear that Margaret started to use that time to tell her husband things she appreciated about him.

We had one more session with Margaret before we saw enough calm in her manner to consider her out of the woods. Her back rarely bothered her. When it did, she knew she was appreciating too little and rushing too much, and she knew how to change her habits. A few follow-up sessions were necessary before we felt comfortable enough with her progress to stop seeing her entirely; she needed booster shots of practice in walking slowly, appreciating the simple things in life, and doing things with attention. At one of those follow-up sessions she admitted that when she got home from her first session with us, she told her husband she had seen two wacky psychologists who had told her to imagine that her cup was half full instead of empty and to slow down. They laughed together, saying, "For that she had to go to Stanford Hospital and see two shrinks!" She told us this by way of introducing what her husband had said to her the previous evening—that those wacky psychologists had sure helped their marriage, and that she should make sure she thanked them for him.

Acknowledgments

We appreciate our peers at the Stanford University School of Medicine who worked with us as we developed the LifeSkills: Dr. William Haskell, Dr. John A. Astin, Kathy Berra, Annette Clark, Shauna Hyde, Linda Klienman, Kelly Reilly, and Pauline Siedenburg.

Among the leaders of American Specialty Health, we would like to thank George DeVries, Dr. Douglas Metz, Dr. Rene Vega, and Wendy Brown for their insights and assistance. Finally, our appreciation goes to the owners and senior management of Canyon Ranch, including Mel Zuckerman, Jerry Cohen, and Dr. Gary Frost.

We thank our agent, Jillian Manus, and our editor, Gideon Weil, for jobs well done.

Fred Luskin could not have completed this book, nor would he have wanted to, without the support of his wonderful family—Jan, Danny, and Anna.

Ken Pelletier, as always, honors his wife, Elizabeth, for her compassion, patience, integrity, and the love they have shared for these many lifetimes.